HIS
VOLUME FIVE

RESCUE
AND
REDEEM

CHRONICLES OF
THE MODERN CHURCH

History Lives
Volume Five

Rescue and Redeem

Chronicles of the Modern Church

MINDY AND
BRANDON WITHROW

CF4•K

© Copyright 2009 Mindy and Brandon Withrow
Reprinted 2010
Christian Focus Publications
ISBN: 978-1-84550-433-5
Published by Christian Focus Publications,
Geanies House, Fearn, Tain, Ross-shire,
IV20 1TW, Scotland, U.K.
www.christianfocus.com
email:info@christianfocus.com

Cover design by Jonathan Williams
Cover illustration by Jonathan Williams
Printed and bound by Norhaven, Denmark

For Aoife and Niamh
and for Kayla, Joshua, and Jovie

May you see God's hand in all things.

Acknowledgments

It would be difficult to sustain the writing of a five-volume series like *History Lives* without people around us to keep us motivated and (mostly) sane. And for that, we must begin by thanking our many nieces and nephews, to whom (with a few honorary ones) these volumes are dedicated. You kept our fingers typing with your unconditional love and spontaneous joy—and supplied us with a writer's lifetime of funny dialogue. We also thank our parents for presenting the message of Christ in our youths. To Mindy's parents, Rex and Tina Rice, who without hesitation opened to us the second floor of their farmhouse for the writing of two volumes (and cooked when we were too busy researching, and assisted with last-minute proofing)—you've been great neighbors! (Hope you're ready for our next project!) And to Brandon's parents, Greg and Carol Withrow, for promoting the series to family, church friends, and random strangers on the phone—keep it coming. Our family-away-from-family in Philadelphia—especially Diana and Jeff Frazier, Mike and Rachel Vendsel, Jen and Joe Troutman, and Mark and Karyn Traphagen—enthusiastically cheered us on. We long for more Fabulous Fridays and never-ending coffee house chats with you!

We are grateful to Catherine Mackenzie, children's editor at Christian Focus, who set us on the path of this rewarding project and graciously (and repeatedly) overlooked our missed deadlines and word choice quibbles. We appreciate the excellent research of Brian Cosby, Brandon's teaching assistant at Beeson Divinity School. We thank Westminster Bookstore in Pennsylvania for vigorously promoting the series. And to Winebrenner Theological Seminary, we are grateful for showcasing the series on campus and giving us an academic community in Ohio.

And, finally, we say thank you to the fans of this series, young and "old," students and teachers and parents, homeschoolers and seminarians alike. Your recommendations, blog reviews, and emails have deeply encouraged us. As the history of Christianity lives on, may it welcome your many future contributions!

CONTENTS

Modern Church Timeline
1860 - TODAY

1860 Abraham Lincoln becomes U.S. president; American Civil War begins

1865 Hudson Taylor founds China Inland Missions; American Civil War ends; Salvation Army founded

1866 Robert Thomas martyred in Korea

1869 First Vatican Council begins

1870 Black males win voting rights in U.S.

1871 Great Chicago Fire destroys city

1874 Niijima Jō becomes first Japanese ordained Protestant minister

1883 D. L. Moody and Ira Sankey lead evangelistic meetings in U.K.

1886 Chicago Evangelism Society (later Moody Bible Institute) formed

1889 Pandita Ramabai establishes Mukti Mission in India

1893 Princess Kaʻiulani pleads for return of Hawaiian sovereignty

1901 England's Queen Victoria dies

1903 Orville and Wilbur Wright make first plane flight

1905 Albert Einstein publishes *Special Theory of Relativity*

1906 Azusa Street Revival launches Pentecostalism

1907 Korean Presbyterian Church formed

1908 Henry Ford introduces Model T; G.K. Chesterton publishes *Orthodoxy*

1910 Edinburgh World Missionary Conference held

1919 Versailles Treaty ends World War I

1920 League of Nations formed; women achieve voting rights in U.S.

1925 "Scopes Monkey Trial" in Tennessee

1928 Women achieve voting rights in England

1932 Karl Barth publishes first volume of *Church Dogmatics*

1938 Gladys Aylward rescues Chinese orphans during Japanese invasion

1940 Wycliffe Bible Translators founded

1942 Marianna Slocum begins translation work in Mexico; National Association of Evangelicals formed in U.S.

1944 Corrie ten Boom arrested by Nazis for hiding Jews

1945 Dietrich Bonhoeffer hanged by Nazis; atomic bombs dropped on Hiroshima and Nagasaki; World War II ends

1947 Dead Sea Scrolls discovered

1948 Billy Graham's first evangelistic crusade; World Council of Churches formed; State of Israel founded; Gandhi assassinated

1949 Communists rise to power in China

1950 First organ transplant; C.S. Lewis publishes first *Narnia* book

1951 Richard Niebuhr publishes *Christ and Culture*

1952 Revised Standard Version published; Elizabeth II crowned

1953 DNA discovered; Joseph Stalin dies

1955 Francis Schaeffer founds L'Abri

1956 Five missionaries martyred in Ecuador

1957 Sputnik 1 becomes first space craft launched

1962 Second Vatican Council begins

1963 John F. Kennedy assassinated; Martin Luther King, Jr. gives "I Have a Dream" speech

1967 Richard and Sabina Wurmbrand launch Voice of the Martyrs

1968 Martin Luther King, Jr. assassinated

1974 Lausanne Congress on World Evangelism held

1977 Janani Luwum, Archbishop of Uganda, martyred by Idi Amin

1978 New International Version published

1981 U.S. launches first Space Shuttle mission

1989 Fall of Berlin Wall

2001 Terrorists attack Twin Towers, Pentagon, and crash a plane in Pennsylvania

2003 Spirit Rover launched to Mars; coalition led by U.S. invades Iraq

2004 Tsunami kills thousands on Indian coast

2005 Terrorists bomb London's public transport system; Hurricane Katrina nearly destroys New Orleans

2007 Twenty-two South Korean missionaries taken hostage in Iraq

What is the Modern Church?

WHEN WE USE the word *modern*, we usually mean something *new*. But since all things are new at one time or another, we need to be more specific when we talk about the *modern church*. In this book, the modern church refers to the period of time starting just before the beginning of the nineteenth century and continuing to today. That's right—*you* are part of the modern church! But you are at the tail end of it, and life was pretty different when this period began. So this book will focus mostly on the early years of the modern church—the part that most of us are less familiar with—and then lead us back to the present day.

Since things were so different at the beginning of the modern period, let's start with a little introduction. The most important thing to keep in mind about this period is that it has been a time of very big and very rapid changes! Christians from every background struggled to apply their faith to the challenges of this ever-changing world.

Remember the eighteenth-century movement called the *Enlightenment*? Enlightenment thinkers emphasized the use of human reason for understanding the universe. They were suspicious of religious authorities, like the Bible and the church. They believed that organized religion was just a human invention and the cause of many of the world's problems. So they argued that if we would just trust in science and education instead of religion, we could build a better world. This was the foundation of the modern period, and people born at the beginning of it grew up thinking this way.

A WORLD OF CHANGES

Since people had a new confidence in their ability to improve the world, they got busy doing it. Things started changing in every area of life. Government changed, because of a push for *democracy* throughout the world. Medicine changed, as our knowledge of science improved—and as it did, the world's population grew. In fact, in the years between 1850 and 1950—just 100 years—the world's population doubled! That meant we had a lot more people to feed, and since old farming methods no longer provided enough food, *agriculture* changed, too. Manufacturing changed when machines were invented that could work faster than humans, and more efficient mills and factories were built. And communities changed, as huge numbers of people began to move from the country into cities, where all the new industry offered them jobs.

As you might guess, this created a new problem. Cities began to *overpopulate*, plunging a lot of people into terrible working and living conditions. The world had never faced a problem quite like this, and the old ways from previous centuries didn't offer any solutions—so once again, people put their heads together and came up with more changes.

Over the next century and a half, the technology available in cities spread into other areas. New forms of transportation provided a way to live outside the city but go back into it every day for work.

So those who could afford it moved out to the suburbs, leaving a generally poorer population living in the cities. As a big part of the workforce moved out to the suburbs, so did manufacturers. Soon cities were no longer the centers of manufacturing, but of business, education, entertainment, and art—and also, unfortunately, centers of violence and poverty. Another new problem!

Again, people called for change. So new laws were passed and *labor unions* formed to protect workers and their families—and to keep industries from taking advantage of a labor force that included a lot of children. And to keep governments responsible, greater rights were given to citizens. But these laws did not erase injustice, which took many forms. Some Christians, who saw these issues ultimately as the result of sin, believed the gospel called them to get involved. In fact, in many cases, it was Christians who led the charge to make sure people were cared for during all these rapid changes.

A SHRINKING WORLD

From the middle of the 1800s to the early years of the new millennium, the world shrank. Well, the planet didn't actually get smaller, but several important inventions made it a lot easier—and faster—to travel and communicate between countries.

Radios, developed at the end of the nineteenth century, led to the first radio station, which began broadcasting in 1920 in Pittsburgh, Pennsylvania. Suddenly, people could talk to each other across great distances.

In 1903, in Kitty Hawk, North Carolina, brothers Orville (1871-1948) and Wilbur (1867-1912) Wright made the first plane flight. Soon, instead of traveling for weeks across the ocean by ship, people were flying to other countries in just a matter of hours. Today, just over a century after the first airplane flight, astronauts live in space and send roving robotic explorers to other planets.

The invention of the computer is another big one. The technology developed to improve computers has provided a lot of other advances in medicine and other sciences. With the rise of the internet in the late twentieth century, people can communicate across the globe instantly. And that has connected local *economies* (financial systems) into a global economy.

Global economy, global internet, global travel—modern Christians realized it would take a global church to cover the world with the gospel.

GLOBAL CHRISTIANITY

The very first Christians were given a mission to "go into all the world and proclaim the gospel to every creature" (Mark 16:15). In the first few centuries of the church, they did this by setting up monastic communities that ministered to their neighbors or by traveling and planting churches. Later, when Christianity became linked with empire, the church grew through military might, like during the Medieval *Crusades,* when organized Christianity was sent abroad—but at the cost of exchanging the gospel of peace for the sword. Similarly, during the *Reformation*, nations went to war over differences between Catholics and Protestants. And in the generations after that, it wasn't just the differences between Catholics and Protestants that caused friction; it was also the differences between Protestants and Protestants.

By the beginning of the modern period, many Christians looked back on those turbulent centuries and longed for—you guessed it!—a change. Some believed that they should only emphasize the essential beliefs of the church so that minor differences would not keep them from working together. They wanted to seek unity instead of division, so some denominations merged together to become a stronger whole with a bigger impact for Christ. Other Christians resisted these efforts to unite, believing it would require them to sacrifice doctrinal purity. Since this would mean they had fewer resources, they focused on one kind of ministry or one part of the world they could effectively reach.

Either way Christians approached it, the effort of thinking through global issues brought about a new perspective on ministering to the world.

What was the new perspective? Christians began to act and think *globally*, meaning they were more aware of other cultures and the needs of people across the planet, not just their own country. And this brought about a new approach to missions. In previous centuries, Western missionaries (missionaries from the Western world, such as Britain and America) who delivered the gospel to foreign lands also delivered their Western culture. Converts were expected to dress and talk like the missionary did. But now, many Christians realized that being a Christian had nothing to do with wearing British or American clothing. It was about living out the gospel in every culture.

And it turns out that sin flourishes around the globe! As Christians arrived for the first time in other countries, they found great injustices that only the gospel could address. So they set out to rescue and redeem their fellow human beings—spiritually *and* physically.

AN ANCIENT GOSPEL FOR A MODERN WORLD

The stories in this book, covering the years from 1860 to the late 1900s, chronicle the labors of global Christians in places as diverse as Japan, China, Korea, the United States, India, Hawai'i, Mexico, Germany, England, Uganda, and on the open seas between them. They are pastors (Dietrich Bonhoeffer, Janani Luwum), royals (Princess Ka'iulani), writers (C.S. Lewis), translators (John Ross and Marianna Slocum), samurai (Niijima Jō), missionaries (Robert Thomas, Samuel Moffet, and Hudson and Maria Taylor), educators (Pandita Ramabai), and evangelists (Dwight Moody and Ira Sankey). These are people who either lived their lives by their convictions or sacrificed their lives for their convictions.

These are stories of real Christians, taken from their diaries, letters, and books. They are told from their own perspectives, showing us how they understood their places in the Christian story. They did not all agree with each other on the teachings of the Bible. They did not all have the same level of influence—some are legendary and others are all but forgotten. They were sometimes wise, sometimes foolish. But they met the challenges of modern life with new ways of communicating the ancient gospel, seeking to be God's tools as he rescued his global people and redeemed them to new life in Christ.

Niijima Jō: No more my parents', but my God's

JULY 17, 1864. HAKODATE, JAPAN.

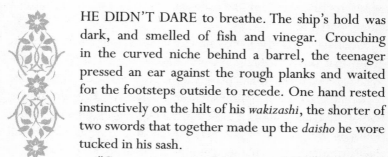

HE DIDN'T DARE to breathe. The ship's hold was dark, and smelled of fish and vinegar. Crouching in the curved niche behind a barrel, the teenager pressed an ear against the rough planks and waited for the footsteps outside to recede. One hand rested instinctively on the hilt of his *wakizashi*, the shorter of two swords that together made up the *daisho* he wore tucked in his sash.

"Courage, samurai," Niijima told himself. "Yes, leaving the country is forbidden on penalty of death. But it will go badly for the captain if he is caught smuggling me out, so he will not let the inspectors discover me."

For a few minutes it was quiet. But just when he thought it might be safe, the customs officers passed by again, shouting questions to the crewmen accompanying them. Cramps gripped his calf muscles, but he held his position, motionless as a statue of the emperor. To distract himself, he took deep breaths and steered his thoughts away from the ship and the unpleasant cargo hold.

Cherry blossoms burst into his mind. Frothy pink clouds of petals draping the trees back in Edo. The *sakura* had been in bloom only weeks before he left home, and he had gone with his family to the grove near their ancestral temple for a traditional viewing party.

Ah, Edo. Sakura blossoms were not the only images that came to mind when he thought of home. He often stood at the window of his room in his grandparents' house and studied the view. Theirs was one of many samurai mansions that circled the center of the city, their quiet gardens and spiral-turned gateposts leading inward toward Edo Castle, the centuries-old home of the *shogun* they served. Each generation of the shogunate had added new rooms and towers to the castle, building up and out in every direction. From Niijima's window view, the castle rose above its walls, layers of curling eaves stacked like plates and cups in a washbasin after a dinner party.

Grains of rice arose in his mind's eye, too. Long, plump, starchy grains that filled the shogun's warehouses along the Great River. When he was little, he had played at the edge of the water, skipping rocks and watching for glimpses of the highest-ranking samurais as they went in and out of all those official buildings. And he stood for hours on the great bridge, where all the ships were unloaded and the fishermen and craftsmen sold their goods or transferred them to barges to sell inland.

He had sketched that bridge many times. Even now, he felt the oily black sticks of charcoal that turned into bridges and trees and people as he put them to paper for his art assignments. And the pots of silky ink into which he dipped his brush in calligraphy class, or to write out mathematical equations for his tutor, or to mark points on the navigation charts he studied.

Navigation. That thought brought him back to the present, to his cramped calves crouched in the cargo hold. It was his study of navigation that stirred up all these ideas of travel and study and foreign lands. He knew people back home would think him a traitor when they discovered he had snuck out of Japan without permission, but the truth was that he was doing it out of loyalty— self-disciplined, samurai loyalty.

He remembered standing on Edo Bridge and catching a glimpse of Dutch warships in the bay. "How stately and formidable they look!" he had exclaimed, though no one was listening. "Next to these dignified sea queens, our Japanese sailing junks are clumsy." The comparison worried him. His duty as a samurai was not just to his shogun, but to the whole nation of Japan. And Japan was surrounded by sea. If their naval force could not match those of other countries, how could they defend themselves? Clearly, it was his duty to learn the art of navigation. His shogun would be proud of him.

But his shogun was too busy to be proud—busy avoiding assassination. When you're a prince, you can't be too careful with your life! He needed bodyguards when he traveled, and he wanted Niijima to be one of them. By this time, Niijima had been studying navigation for months. The shogun didn't seem to think his studies were important, at least not compared to checking his bathroom or balcony for potential assassins. Niijima began to feel more like a slave than a samurai. But he was loyal—to his shogun and to his family.

He was always seeking his parents' approval. After all, he was a samurai who lived by principles of dignity and honor. He rose early in the morning and walked over three miles to his family's temple to receive a blessing from their god. He observed the days of his ancestors, and went to their graves to worship their spirits. His father and his father's father were also samurai, and any shame he brought on himself would be a disgrace to them, too. So he had no choice but to go when his prince called, and fit his studies into his off-duty hours.

But he hadn't forgotten the view of those Dutch warships, and when the opportunity arose to study the Dutch language, he accepted eagerly.

"Your prince is generous to permit these lessons," his tutor remarked after a few weeks of study. They were meeting in the tutor's house, one of the old samurai homes on the far side of the castle.

"When he is at home and doesn't need as many bodyguards, he is very generous with my time," Niijima shrugged. Complaining would get him nowhere.

But the old tutor noticed the frown on the young samurai's face. He got up, hobbled to a sagging bookshelf, and took down a hefty volume. "Your language skills are coming along well. To congratulate you, you may borrow a book."

"What is it?"

"There are other, perhaps more interesting, things to read than grammar books." He passed the book across the table. "The best Japanese translation I could find."

Niijima glanced at the cover. "'Robinson Crusoe?' What does that mean?"

"It is a man's name," said the tutor. "A man who has a great adventure. I think his story will suit you."

The young man lowered his head in a demonstration of humility. "I will read it with interest," he said. But he suspected it would bore him. What did an old tutor know of adventure?

But he was wrong. He was off-duty again the next day, and opened the book after breakfast. Soon his eyes were wide with delight. Sea voyages! Pirates! Shipwreck! Escaped prisoners! He was enthralled with Crusoe's adventures and didn't stop reading until he had turned the last page.

He immediately loaned it to his grandfather. He was looking forward to talking to someone about the book, and if anyone liked a good story, it was Grandfather. But when the old samurai called him into his sitting room, he didn't look excited. He was frowning, and tapping his bony fingers on the carved head of his walking stick.

"Such books are dangerous, young one," he said, after his grandson greeted him with a proper bow. "I fear this will mislead you."

Niijima could not hide his disappointment. "How, Grandfather?"

"Crusoe makes it sound like an adventure. But consider what hardships he endured, all because he left his parents! An honorable samurai would not do such a thing."

Niijima wondered if Grandfather suspected how unhappy he was in his service to the prince. He decided to take a risk. "Yes, Grandfather. But Crusoe became educated in the ways of the world. He gained knowledge and experience for his people. He learned to be a warrior."

Grandfather tugged at his goatee, many inches long and streaked with white. "Your father is a warrior, and he did not leave Japan and his family to become one. He would wield his sword for the prince if it was necessary."

But he doesn't wield a sword, Niijima thought, he wields a pen. His father was a bureaucrat, a record keeper for the shogun. And so was Niijima, except for the occasions when he traveled as the prince's bodyguard. He had been appointed an assistant in the records office on his fourteenth birthday, the day of the ceremony that marked his transition from boy to man. He and his father dressed as their soldier ancestors, with their long hair tied into topknots and their swords tucked into their sashes. But most samurai these days did paperwork. It had been many years since a battle between shoguns required their knights to exercise fighting skills.

"Honor and duty to the shogun first and then to our fellow samurai," Grandfather was saying. "That includes your family."

Niijima acknowledged his honor and duty by giving Grandfather another polite bow and slipping the book into the waistband of his trousers. He would take it back to his tutor. But it was too late to forget what he had read. The idea of a sea voyage to exotic lands had firmly lodged in his brain.

He began to read every foreign book he could find, books about the United States and a history of the world by a British missionary. The descriptions of other countries stirred him. He longed to leave Japan—not forever, just long enough to discover what else was out there—but how could he leave his family?

And then among some Chinese books, he found a curious one about another book called the Bible. Who is this creator they call "Heavenly Father"? he wondered. He believed in honoring and even worshiping his ancestors—after all, they had brought him into being—but none of them had created the world. Yet this book spoke of an almighty creator God who called people his sons and daughters. "If I am one of this Heavenly Father's sons, and so are all of my ancestors," he thought, "then this God deserves my worship even more than they do!"

He read on with growing interest, discovering that this creator called people to follow him and promised to provide what they needed to serve him. He closed the book as a new realization dawned on him. "I have always thought that my first duty is to my family," he reasoned aloud. "But if this book is true, then even if I leave my earthly father, I have a Heavenly Father who is with me wherever I go. I am no more my parents', but my God's! My duty is to him first. I must go wherever he calls me."

But just where was he being called? "The only way to learn more about this Heavenly Father and discover Japan's place in the world is to leave my country," he decided. The idea was scary, but also exciting. And the opportunity soon presented itself.

One day he ran into a friend, a fellow samurai who served another prince. The friend was helping his prince find navigators to take his schooner to the port at Hakodate, and he knew that Niijima had been studying navigation. He introduced Niijima to his prince, who immediately made arrangements with the other prince to hire the young samurai.

Niijima couldn't believe he finally was going to navigate a ship. It was an adventure to make Robinson Crusoe proud! Then, soberly, he realized that Hakodate was an international port. Once he was there, chances were good that he could board an international ship and sneak out of the country.

He told his family about the job. When they asked, he said it was a round trip and that the ship would return after a few weeks. His parents said they were proud of his achievement. But they smiled like they were sad, and Grandfather wouldn't look him in the eye. And when they prepared a feast in his honor the night before his departure, he knew for certain that they suspected his plans.

At the end of the feast, Father passed him the *mizu sakazuki*, a cup of cold water drunk by a person leaving on a long journey. Niijima said nothing, but accepted it and drank. Then Grandfather stood and put his hand on his grandson's shoulder.

"It is traditional to write a haiku to bless a traveler," he said. "So here is my poem for Niijima. *Ikeru nara / Itte mite ko yo / Hana no yama*. If you can manage it, go seek the mountain of flowers, and come back."

Niijima rose and bent low before his grandfather. He knew the message was meant to say, "Take courage and go your own way, but don't forget where you came from."

And so he did. But it wasn't easy. As he navigated the schooner up the coast toward Hakodate, the samurai remembered his mother's tears when she said good-bye. He told himself that if he saw the world and brought back crucial knowledge for Japan, she would take comfort that her sacrifice had not been in vain. He wouldn't let her down. Someday he would return in glory!

The day the ship docked in Hakodate, he set his plan in motion. He had no relatives there, and he didn't want to stay in a hotel where the staff might notice his disappearance later. So when he heard about a foreigner who might have an extra room for him, he followed the directions straight to a small chapel. Several foreigners were on their way out of the building, and he stepped aside in the narrow garden so they could pass him.

The man who met him in the doorway was unlike any he had seen. Fair skinned, bearded, and brightly clothed, he looked about ten years older than the samurai. He carried a basket, and Niijima noticed a silver cup and a lacquered box peeking out of silk wrappings.

"How can I help you, samurai?" the man asked in poor Japanese.

"I was told you are from Russia."

"Yes. My name is Nicholai. I am an Orthodox priest."

The teenager squinted at him in confusion.

"A Christian teacher," the priest explained, "in the Russian church."

A Christian teacher! Why, this man would know about the Heavenly Father! Niijima broke into a broad grin. "Pleased to meet you," he said. He put a hand on his chest and pronounced his name slowly and loudly for the foreigner's benefit. "Will you teach me English and give me a place to stay? I can instruct you in better Japanese."

Nicholai laughed, rubbing the back of his head in embarrassment. "I have been here three years, but still I struggle with your language." He smiled. "It is very different from Russian, you know! But I had been thinking of hiring another tutor, and I do have a spare room in my lodgings. If you are willing to do it—."

"You will teach me English?"

"Well, I'm not that good with English either. But I have a friend who is very good, and I can get him to teach you."

"I would be grateful."

"This is a providential meeting, then," said the priest, moving toward the garden. "Come. I'll show you my house."

For the next few weeks, they exchanged language lessons. Nicholai's friend taught Niijima how to say basic English phrases, and Niijima helped Nicholai practice Japanese. In the evenings, the samurai and the priest often sat together at home reading aloud passages from the Kojiki, an ancient holy book, so the priest could learn more about Japanese religious traditions. In turn, the priest explained his Christian traditions, answering Niijima's questions about the Heavenly Father and his one son, called Christ, who was so different from the others like Niijima that were also called his children.

Then Niijima started to accompany Nicholai during the day as the priest went about his work. The Russian missionary and his colleagues were busy setting up hospitals and providing free medical care to the sick and elderly. Niijima was impressed by the missionaries' kindness and generosity. He thought they were doing it to build a good reputation for Russia. Since few foreigners were allowed into Japan and few Japanese people were allowed out, he figured that if the Japanese princes saw the Russians aiding the poor, maybe they would be more open to interacting with Russia. A good thing for everybody, he thought. But eventually he discovered that the Russian priest had a bigger goal than international politics.

"I thought foreigners were not allowed to make Christians from the Japanese people," Niijima objected when Nicholai revealed his real purpose for being in Japan.

They were sitting on the floor in a quiet tea room not far from the chapel where they had met. The low table between them was only big enough to hold the hot teapot on its trivet and two tiny matching cups. Soft light filtering through the rice paper walls and the slow-rising vapors of steam gave them a feeling of privacy.

Nicholai nodded at his companion. "Technically, it is against the law to make converts, yes. We're allowed to worship with other foreigners. And we're allowed to minister to the locals with medicine or alms, but legally we are not to convert them to a foreign religion. But tell me, samurai"——he had started to lift his cup but set it down again——"if a local asks me why I minister, am I not obligated to tell him the truth? So I answer that I do it to serve Jesus Christ. And then, of course, he wants to know more."

"You welcome danger?" Niijima leaned forward, wondering how a foreigner could understand samurai principles of truth and honor.

"Not for the sake of danger itself, no. But I believe that Christ is the savior of the world. Without him, a person's soul is in eternal danger, and that is far worse than my legal risks."

"So you came to Japan to tell my people about Christ?"

"I was commissioned by the Czar of Russia himself! But, so far, I have taught many people without converting anyone. They are afraid the change of religion will separate them from their families." Nicholai filled both of their cups. "Niijima, we have talked some about Christianity. But I don't think you realize just how different and powerful this religion is from the one your people follow. Tell me, what exactly do you know of Christianity?"

"I have read a few Chinese books that speak of the creator and the son and the dove. I have learned from you that this son is called Christ and that he is to be worshiped with the Father. I know the Heavenly Father is with me wherever I go, and that duty to him comes before other duties. I know that Christians like you believe it is your duty to care for the poor."

"But you do not know of the cross, of resurrection, of baptism?"

The samurai blinked with confusion. The Chinese books he had read said more details were written in a book called the Bible, but he had not yet found that book.

Nicholai looked him in the eye. "My people were once like yours, knowing nothing of Christ and his gospel. We used to worship gods we made with our own hands. But, almost 900 years ago, our Prince Vladimir brought back the Christian religion he discovered in a place called Constantinople. Now many Russians worship the true God who sacrificed his son so we could have eternal life. And he calls us to take his message to the whole world."

Niijima looked into his tea, letting the fragrant steam sort out his thoughts. "Japanese people need a moral reformation, a change in our beliefs," he said after a moment. "The more I learn about Christ and his Heavenly Father, the more I think that such change must come through Christianity."

Nicholai glanced toward the door, but they were still the only customers. He said quietly, "Do you plan to be the one who brings this change?"

The samurai followed his friend's glance, assuring himself no one would hear. "Yes," he answered in a low voice. "I plan to leave the country and visit the West. I have much to learn there for Japan's sake, including the Christian faith."

"Then you are the one that welcomes danger!" replied the priest. "You could be killed if you were caught leaving the country."

"But, like you, I must obey the Heavenly Father first. I came to Hakodate for this purpose, and everything you have told me confirms that I must go through with my plan."

"Then you are welcome to stay with me for as long as you are in Hakodate. I would like to teach you more about Christ before you go."

Over the following weeks, Niijima continued his English lessons and studied Christian doctrine with Nicholai. He was now convinced, like Nicholai, that Christ was the savior of the world and that it was his duty to tell others about him. But there was so much more he needed to learn! And he had not yet been able to find a Bible in Japanese or Chinese, the two languages he could read, and he longed to read it for himself. It was time for him to continue his journey.

He realized he would draw less attention on the street if he did not dress as a samurai, so he put his sash and his *daisho* away in Nicholai's house and cut his hair to his shoulders. Then he started making quiet inquiries into ships bound for other countries. For a bribe, a wrinkled clerk who worked with English-speaking merchants found an American ship whose captain was willing to take him as far as China.

The night Niijima was to leave, Nicholai was away on a trip. He made his final preparations in the quiet house. He put his borrowed room in order, packed his *daisho* carefully in his bag, and wrote a letter to his parents. He posted the letter on his way to the docks. By the time he got there it was fully dark, and he let the smell of the sea and the creaking of water-logged pilings lead him to the right place. The clerk was waiting for him in a dinghy.

Niijima was about to say hello when he was startled by a dog barking close by. In the dark, the whites of the clerk's eyes widened suddenly in alarm.

"Your shoes!" the clerk whispered hoarsely. "You made too much noise! Quick, in the boat."

Niijima dove into the dinghy, setting it to violent rocking.

"Who's there?" came a shout from the shore.

He flattened himself against the boat's rolling bottom and covered his chest and face with his bag. A vicious growl sounded somewhere above him.

The clerk grabbed for the line, still tied to the dock, to steady the dinghy. "Over here," he declared, as the watchman and his dog appeared out of the darkness. "I have business with the American captain that cannot wait until morning."

The dog sniffed the ropes, stopped growling, and sat down on the dock.

"Oh, it's you," said the watchman. He peered down into the boat at the small pile of packages. "Next time, alert one of us if you intend to row out to the ships. We can't be responsible for the dogs, you know."

"Of course," said the clerk. "My apologies. Well, good night." He lifted the lines, picked up the oars, and began rowing out into the bay.

Niijima shoved his bag from his chest. "Sorry," he whispered, when they were far enough out. "Robinson Crusoe never would have made such a mistake."

"What?" the clerk hissed back. "You better be more careful, or you'll never get out of this bay!"

A quarter hour later, Niijima climbed up a rope ladder to the deck of the *Berlin*. The captain was waiting for him and started talking as soon as he swung his feet over the side.

"Welcome aboard, mister," he said briskly, drawing Niijima below decks. "We need to discuss terms, but looks like we're about to get a visit from your friendly customs inspectors. Can't afford for them to catch me with you, so your first night on ship will have to be in here." He threw open the cargo hold and shoved his passenger inside. "Stay quiet."

The bolt rang in the lock, followed by the muffled clatter of the captain's boots on the stairs. The only thing thicker than the darkness was the oily smell of salted fish. The castaway held his nose and waited for his eyes to adjust. The stacked crates and rows of barrels told him he was in a secondary cargo hold where the crew stored their food supplies. He was just starting to orient himself when he heard the customs officers come aboard above him.

Crouching in the dark alcove, he let his mind wander. Cherry blossoms. Edo Castle. His first navigation chart. Grandfather's haiku. Nicholai's Russian-accented Japanese as they talked about Christ. The memories kept quiet company as he waited for the inspection to end.

Sometime later, the scrape of the door roused him from cramped sleep. A sailor was unlocking the hold, telling him they had been cleared for departure and were now moving out of the bay. Niijima followed him above decks, where a slash of pink on the horizon announced dawn. He longed to stretch his legs and thanked the captain three times when he invited him to climb the rigging. He couldn't be coaxed down until the sun had risen over the receding mountains of Japan. "Please, Heavenly Father, let me see those beautiful peaks again someday," he kept thinking.

"I'm a fair man," the captain said when his stowaway was planted firmly on deck again. "Everyone on the *Berlin* does their share of the work. The mate will make your assignment and I expect your cooperation. Understood?"

"Thank you, Captain." He bowed in respect but the seaman shooed him toward the mate's cabin.

"Laundry," is all the mate said. He handed him a brush and pointed to a toppling pile of underclothes.

"Oh, this can't be what the captain had in mind," Niijima began to object. "He has accounts to tally or navigation charts to record! After all——."

But the mate was halfway across deck, shouting at a deckhand about one of the sails. The captain was nowhere to be seen.

"After all, I'm a samurai!" he grumbled. He stared at the scrub brush as though an insult was scrawled on the handle. "I hire someone else to wash my own clothes!"

But quickly the thought pierced him that he was fulfilling this part of his mission only by the captain's mercy. The man had risked his livelihood to get him out of Japan. Wrinkling his nose, he squatted in front of the pile and gingerly lifted the first garment between his thumb and forefinger.

The next day, the mate sent him to the galley to wash dishes. Again, he seethed with irritation and muttered to himself as he scrubbed. He was so distracted, he didn't realize he had missed an item in the basin until he saw the flash of a spoon in the torrent of dirty dishwater he was dumping over the rail.

The steward working with him saw it, too. "The captain will beat you for that," he warned.

Niijima panicked. "Was it an expensive silver spoon?" he wondered. "Why would someone put an heirloom in the dish basin?"

He dashed back to his bunk for his money pouch. In the captain's cabin, in broken English, he stuttered out an explanation, begging for pardon and offering to pay for the priceless utensil now lost. But the captain just burst into laughter.

Niijima's face reddened. "Captain?"

"Put your money away," the captain said, closing the samurai's fist around the handful of paper. "The steward was just having a little fun with you. Teasing," he said, drawing out the word to make sure his foreign passenger got the meaning. He chuckled again. "A spoon! Ha!"

Niijima smiled with relief. "Ah, teasing," he repeated.

He went back to work, an awkward feeling in his chest. Doing menial work, being laughed at—in only two days he had learned that on this ship there was no such thing as nobility. But it would take a third lesson for him to realize just how different life outside of Japan was going to be.

The passage to China would take only a few days, but he got a crewman who spoke English to agree to help him practice. This language required sounds foreign to his native Japanese, and they were difficult to pronounce just right. The crewman quickly grew frustrated with his attempts.

"It's not as hard as you're making it," complained the crewman. "Do it again, like this!" He grabbed Niijima's face with both hands to force his mouth into the right shape.

Niijima shoved him away, indignant. "In Japan, a samurai can cut down any man who disrespects him in the street!" he shouted. "I will not be treated this way!"

He charged toward his bunk where he had stored his *daisho*. But when he reached it, the blood pumping in his ears, he suddenly saw his hands on the two swords and realized what he was about to do. Groaning, he threw himself on his cot.

"There is no turning back from such an action," he chided himself. "And this is just a trifling humiliation! If I let my pride control me now, how will I survive all the unknown things to come on my adventure?" He turned over the swords in his hands. "I may be a samurai, but mine is no longer a samurai world. I must turn away from things that will hinder my mission."

He replaced the *daisho* in his luggage. "Patience," he murmured. "The Heavenly Father is with you."

By the end of the week they had anchored in Shanghai. His last night on board, he had cut his hair again, even shorter this time, parting it in the center and tucking the sides behind his ears. He had tossed the black trimmings overboard, asking the sea to carry them back to his family. "I will not grow my hair again in the way of the samurai until I have succeeded in my mission and returned to Japan," he promised the dark waves.

In Shanghai, the crew busied themselves shouting at dockworkers. The *Berlin* was picking up a new load of cargo—Niijima had heard they were expecting large quantities of silk and tea—to deliver back to Hakodate. From the southern pier where they were docked, the port extended in a long half-circle of deep river. He had never seen so many foreigners in one place. The flags of Britain, Japan, and the United States dotted ship masts all along the watery curve.

Niijima knew nobody in Shanghai. But the *Berlin's* captain had taken interest in his unusual stowaway, and offered him some final assistance.

"Samurai, meet Captain Horace Taylor of the *Wild Rover*," he said, steering him toward a weathered man on the other end of the pier.

The man pumped Niijima's hand in a friendly shake. "I understand you're headed to the United States, young man. What's your name?"

He told him, and the captain tried to repeat it back, but the accent was all wrong.

"No, like this." He said it again, slower this time.

"Pardon my Massachusetts ears, son. Do you mind if I just call you Joe? Short for Joseph, a good man in the Bible."

Niijima hesitated, but it was his new policy not to let little things get in the way of his mission. And this man had heard of the

Bible! Plus this gave him a chance to use an English word he had learned on the *Berlin*. "Okay," he said, emphasizing both syllables.

"Okay!" The captain grinned. "I'm willing to take you aboard, Joe, but we have a lot of ports to call on before we get to the States. And I expect you to pay for your passage by working on the ship. Do we have a deal?"

Niijima grimaced at the idea of more dirty laundry and crusty dishes. But it would get him closer to his goal, he reminded himself. So he nodded.

"I understand you're educated, and I could use some responsible help. So you'll work for me personally. Keep my cabin straightened, organize my charts, that sort of thing."

Niijima smiled broadly now. "Okay!"

"Well, then," said Captain Taylor, cocking his head toward the *Wild Rover*, "welcome aboard, Joe!"

The *Wild Rover* became Niijima's home for the next several months as it crossed the seas from Shanghai to Hong Kong to Saigon. Along the way, he studied English, wishing he could study the Bible, too. In Saigon he tried to buy a Chinese New Testament, but found that his Japanese money had no value here. Since he was working for his passage, he had no way to earn local currency—unless he traded something.

He ran back to the ship and pulled his *katana*, the longer sword, from his baggage. Soon he was knocking on Captain Taylor's cabin door.

"I thought you'd gone ashore, Joe," the captain said, inviting him in.

"I did. I wanted to buy a Bible, but I have no money. Please, would you buy my sword? For eight dollars, I can go back and purchase a New Testament."

Captain Taylor reached into his pocket and counted out a few paper bills. "A sword is worth more on the high seas than a Bible. I sure hope you enjoy the reading."

Niijima placed his sword reverently on the captain's table and accepted the money. "I will, Captain. Thank you." He turned to go.

"Oh, Joe," said the seaman, returning to his chair. "Are you, by any chance, interested in helping me navigate? I could use an extra hand at the wheel."

Niijima couldn't agree fast enough. A Bible and a job worthy of his skills, and both in the same day!

The ship sailed again, this time for Manila, and then finally set out toward Boston. Working together, the two men became friends. Niijima told the captain about his dreams for Japan's future and about his pursuit of the Heavenly Father. He also spent a lot of time reading his new Bible and praying that he could find someone to explain it all to him.

The long voyage was full of adventures. He saw a water spout for the first time, climbed the rigging to watch for pirates, and felt the spray of an enormous whale as she surfaced and then crashed back into the depths. When they passed the Cape of Good Hope, the captain told him they were getting close. The distant mountains reminded Niijima of the home he had left behind.

Before they reached the harbor, Captain Taylor dropped anchor and rowed out to meet a fishing boat. "The country has been in civil war, you know," he explained. "I want to know the status before we head in."

Civil war! Niijima had not expected this kind of complication. He paced the deck until the captain returned.

"It's good news and bad," he told the crew. "The good news is that the war is over."

The deckhands cheered.

"But the bad news—the bad news is that President Lincoln has been assassinated."

The samurai knew nothing of this President Lincoln, but the somber faces told him all he needed.

The captain cleared his throat. "We make port in Boston as planned. Bring her about."

Niijima stayed on deck as the sailors scurried to sail the *Wild Rover* into Boston Harbor. He watched the coastline grow larger as they approached, until small islands and anchored ships filled the foreground. Beyond the forest of ship masts, the hills were covered with green fir trees, as straight and sharp as arrows. Gulls screeched and wheeled overhead.

He felt a hand on his shoulder. "Your new home, Joe," the captain said softly. "I guess your Heavenly Father watched over you."

Hours later, while he was straightening Captain Taylor's cabin for the last time, a crewman brought Niijima a message to meet the captain out on the pier. He was waiting with another man, who seemed to be sizing up Niijima as he approached.

"Hello, Joseph," the man said. "Captain Taylor has been telling me you want to study here, especially Bible training. Maybe return to your country as a missionary."

"Yes, sir," Niijima replied, glancing at the captain. "Japan has many needs, especially Christian teaching. I hope to learn much to take back to my people."

The man continued to scan him and then stepped forward, apparently satisfied. "I've known Taylor for many years, and he's a good judge of character." He thrust out a big hand. "I'm Alpheus Hardy. Welcome to America, Joseph!"

"Hardy is a friend of mine, Joe," said the captain. "He's generous and has some influence in these parts. He's willing to help you get a place to live and get into an American school where you can begin your training. You won't make a better friend in Boston."

Niijima gave the man a dignified samurai bow. "Then I am very pleased to meet you!"

Mr. Hardy met him at the ship later that afternoon and took him out for his first American meal, fried fish and clams and boiled potatoes at a pub near the pier.

"Let me show you around town," Mr. Hardy said when they were finishing eating. "What would you like to see first?"

"A place to buy books, please, Mr. Hardy."

The man gave a startled laugh. "A bookshop?"

Niijima nodded.

"All right then, Joe. I think we're going to get along just fine. Let's go find your bookseller, and then I'll introduce you to some Christian friends who will be thrilled to meet you."

They strode down the main street, Niijima staying close at Hardy's side and gazing in wonder at the strange, boxy buildings. They soon located a shop where leather volumes lined the window. A bell over the door jangled as they stepped inside, startling him, but the sight of all those books in English was thrilling. It took the shopkeeper only a moment to find the right one. And the samurai stepped back out into his new world with his very own English copy of *Robinson Crusoe*.

After being introduced to Christ by the Russian Orthodox priest, Niijima gave up his ancestor worship and embraced Christianity. Determined to learn as much as he could about the Bible, he began formal studies as soon as he arrived in the U.S. In this he was greatly assisted by Alpheus and Susan Hardy, a Protestant couple with hearts for missions. They paid his way through Amherst College and Andover Theological Seminary, making him the first Japanese person to graduate from a Western institution of higher learning, and, in 1874, the first Japanese ordained Protestant minister. In gratitude to the couple who treated him like a son, Niijima officially changed his name to Joseph Hardy Neesima.

After a decade of Christian training, he returned to Japan in 1875 as a missionary and educator. By that time, the emperor had consolidated his power, the shogunate had come to an end, and his hometown of Edo had been renamed Tokyo. He reunited with his parents, who later became Christians, and spent the rest of his life establishing a modern education system in Japan and spreading the Christian message. The beginning of his work was the founding of a Protestant college, Doshisha University, in Kyoto. He died in 1890.

Meanwhile, Nicholai, the Russian Orthodox priest, persisted at his mission in Hakodate. He eventually made his first convert, Takuma Sawabe, a Shinto priest sent to assassinate him, who was so changed by Nicholai's message that he later became a missionary, too.

Missions in a Modern World

IN A RAPIDLY-CHANGING world, methods of doing something—anything—are likely to be revised. Christian missions are no exception. During the modern period, missions have changed dramatically in two important ways: they have become more *international* and more *ecumenical*. Let's start with the first category.

AN INTERNATIONAL MISSIONARY EXPLOSION
During the early Reformation, Protestant and Catholic missionaries saw missions as a matter of converting others within their nations to their particular confessions. But eventually, they began to see the need to go to other parts of the world. The *Jesuits*, for example, were very productive Catholic missionaries, like Francis Xavier (1506-1552), who traveled to both India and Japan. In response to Catholic missions, Protestants such as John Calvin (1509-1564) and his church in Geneva sent out their own missionaries to places like Brazil. But these missionary travels were still not commonplace.

In the years leading up to the modern period, Evangelical missionary William Carey (1761-1834)—often called the father of modern missions—published an influential book calling Christians to be more concerned than ever before with *international missions*. This resulted in an explosion of activity over the following decades in the number of Evangelical missionary societies organized to send people around the world. Among the first of these organizations were the *Wesleyan Missionary Society* (1813), the *American Baptist Missionary Union* (1814), and the *Berlin Missionary Society* (1824). And as explorers of the late 1800s and early 1900s went deep into the largest continents and discovered new people groups who had never heard of Christ, these and many other missionary societies responded.

Adventurous missionaries now traveled the world—but missions work was far from easy or safe. Missionaries often did not see eye-to-eye with other missionaries, or with their sending organizations. And when missionaries tied their work too closely to their own culture or to military or commerce, they encountered difficulties.

Robert Jermain Thomas (1839–1866) desired to work in Korea, but the Korean king had closed his country to foreigners, and Thomas's mission society would not send him there. Heading out on his own initiative, Thomas was willing to do whatever it took to get into the country. He became an interpreter for some businessmen who refused the Korean government's warning to leave—an unwise alliance that eventually led to his death.

J. Hudson (1832-1905) and Maria (1837-1870) Taylor founded *China Inland Mission* in 1865 because they were convinced of the need to go deep inland to the most un-evangelized parts of China, places often ignored by other mission societies. And while many of their colleagues insisted that native converts look and act like the missionaries, the Taylors insisted that being a Christian had nothing to do with bonnet styles and what kind of food they ate. They wore traditional Chinese clothing and adopted a Chinese lifestyle so that cultural differences would not get in the way of the gospel.

Despite the challenges, the explosion of missionary activity around the modern world reflects just how "small" the world was becoming. Many missionaries wrote about their travels, and though these books sometimes exaggerated details out of sheer excitement, they were read by more and more people. And in this way, their stories of their work raised even greater interest in taking the gospel to unreached millions.

ECUMENICAL MISSIONS

In addition to being more international, the second big change in modern missions is its *ecumenical* character. If you are ecumenical, you strive for unity with other Christians.

In the years before the beginning of the modern period, many Protestant missionary societies were formed by specific denominations, such as *The Presbyterian Board of Foreign Missions*. These societies often required their missionaries to agree to the doctrines taught by that denomination, and only churches of that denomination supported those missionaries. But there were some missionary organizations, like the *London Missionary Society*, that brought together Congregationalists, Presbyterians, Methodists, and Anglicans to work together in Asia and Africa. And by the end of the nineteenth century, most Protestants concluded that the huge task of world evangelism required them to work together. There was so much to learn about other cultures, and larger numbers of people working together had greater resources to work with. By working together, they hoped to reach greater numbers of people, develop more accurate Bible translations, and offer better schools and hospitals. Calls for Protestant unity were stronger than ever before.

And in 1910, these calls led to the formation of the famous *Edinburgh World Missionary Conference*. The conference was led by

Evangelical John R. Mott (1865-1955), who dedicated his life to missions after spending time at Dwight Moody's summer conference in Massachusetts in 1886. The 1,200 conference members were almost entirely Western, mostly British and American. It was a promising start, and Mott went on to form the *International Missionary Council* in 1921. More global in its approach, half the delegates at the 1928 meeting were from Asia, Africa, and Latin America. The emphasis of this council was on creating *indigenous* churches (churches led by natives of those countries) and getting the church to fight against injustice.

In the twentieth century, the work of international missions was closely tied to large-scale ecumenical efforts. The devastating global effects of World War I led to the formation of *The League of Nations* (1920-1946). Similarly, in 1920 the Holy Synod of the Church of Constantinople called for a "league" of churches, but it was delayed by World War II so the *World Council of Churches* did not officially form until 1948. In 1961, Mott's International Missionary Council merged with the World Council of Churches and became its Division on World Mission and Evangelism.

But not all Evangelicals could align themselves with the World Council of Churches. In the United States, the *National Association of Evangelicals*, which had formed in 1942, decided to create an international organization like the World Council of Churches but that would be limited to Evangelicals only. When it formed in 1951, it was called the *World Evangelical Fellowship*. And in 1974, Evangelicals of various denominations formed *The Lausanne Congress on World Evangelization*, led by Billy Graham and with delegates from 150 countries, including Ugandan Archbishop Janani Luwum.

And ecumenical groups continue to form for the cause of the gospel. Many of these represent specific theological traditions, like the *World Reformed Fellowship*, which formed in 1994 and has board members from eighteen nations.

Today, with South Korea sending more foreign missionaries than any other country except the United States, missions is no longer primarily the work of Western countries, but is truly international! The modern period has seen a serious transformation of how Christians work with each other to proclaim the gospel around the globe.

HUDS⊕N AND ⅢARIA TAYL⊕R: T⊕ CHINA'S PERISHING ⅢILLI⊕NS

MAY 2, 1866. LONDON, ENGLAND.

BLUE-GRAY WAVES LAPPED at the heavy pilings, gently rocking the dock with a rhythmic creaking. The young man facing the water ran a hand over the broad ropes looped between the posts. They were stiff with salt spray and bristly, leaving fibrous splinters in the tips of his fingers.

A briny breeze lifted his hair from the peak high on his forehead, a feeling that roused memories of his last sea voyage. "How can six years pass so quickly?" he thought. "How much has China changed since I left?"

When he first went to that faraway land, he was a new Christian and an even newer missionary. When he returned to England a few years later, he brought home a deeper desire to minister to the Chinese people, a better knowledge of their culture, and a wife who was equally dedicated to missionary work. The two of them had spent the last six years in England preparing to go back to China for good. Now that he had finished his medical training, he could barely contain his desire to set foot in China again.

"So which one is ours?," he murmured aloud, scanning the ships bobbing restlessly in the harbor. His eyes settled on a full-rigged iron clipper ship. "Ah, there she is—the *Lammermuir*."

Slipping a hand into his vest pocket, he felt for the crisp edge of an envelope. He rubbed it between his fingers for reassurance.

"Mr. Hudson Taylor?"

He turned.

"The name's Bell, Captain Bell," said the man behind him. His right arm was extended to offer a handshake.

Hudson accepted with a firm grip, saying, "Good to meet you, Mr. Bell."

"I understand some special arrangements have been made?"

He pulled the envelope from his pocket and tapped one short end until a folded sheet dropped from the other. "I received a letter this morning from the shipping agents, Messrs. Killick Martin and Co., notifying me of a generous donation to our missions agency. They have offered us the entire passenger accommodation of the *Lammermuir* for our party's voyage to China." He unfolded the sheet of writing paper and held it out to the captain.

But Bell waved it away. "They sent me a copy. How many passengers are in your party?"

"Sixteen missionaries," he answered, tucking the letter back in his coat, "but including my children and their nursemaid, there are 22 of us in all."

"With my crew, that will put us at just over 50. An adequate number for this ship."

Hudson followed his gaze to the *Lammermuir*. "She's a beauty."

"She is," Bell nodded in agreement, "and trustworthy, too. She can take a beating—which is good, considering how rough the China Sea can get this time of year. It is a four-month journey, but we'll have room to stock plenty of supplies, and we may also make a couple stops along the way."

"Sounds fine."

Bell turned to face him and leaned back against the heavy looping ropes. "So which mission organization is sending you to China? The London Missionary Society? The China Evangelization Society?"

Hudson tilted his head. "You're familiar with missions work, Mr. Bell?"

The captain shrugged. "My first mate is what you might call a 'true believer.' And it's not all that uncommon for one of my passengers to be a burdened soul hoping to change the world by preaching his religion in some God-forsaken land."

"I see," Hudson said with a smile. "Well, I'm quite sure you've never heard of our agency—but I do hope you'll hear a lot more about it in the future. You see, we have recently formed our own."

"Oh? Good for you," Bell said. But doubt flickered behind his eyes.

Hudson's smile only broadened. "I know, you're wondering how we will survive if no one has heard of us to give us money. It's an honest question, Mr. Bell. But I never have trouble remembering that my children need breakfast and dinner, so I find it hard to believe God would forget about his children either."

Bell pushed off the ropes and glanced toward the other end of the docks. "Well, sounds like you have a plan, Mr. Taylor. And you'll be working in Shanghai?"

"No."

The unexpected answer drew Bell's distracted gaze back to Hudson's face.

"We're stopping in Shanghai only long enough to take on supplies," the missionary said. "Our real destination is the interior."

Now it was curiosity that glimmered in the captain's eyes.

"There are millions of Chinese men and women who haven't heard the gospel yet," Hudson explained. "We don't want to cover the same territory as every other missionary who ever set foot in China. Shanghai was once devoid of the gospel, but a number of churches have been built there now. We want to go where no Christian has gone before. That means trekking deep into the interior."

Bell stuck out his hand again. "Well, I wish you success, Mr. Taylor. We depart on the 26th of this month. Prior to that, I will need a passenger list from you as well as a list of particular cargo needs."

"I'll see that you get the information," Hudson agreed, pumping his hand.

"Remember," Bell said, as he turned to go, "my job ends as soon as you reach Chinese soil."

Hudson laughed. "We won't expect you to go inland with us, but if you change your mind on the voyage, we'll be glad to consider your application to missionary work!"

The captain shot him a good-natured grimace and hurried on with his business.

The following day, Hudson called a meeting of his fellow missionaries. They were to join him and his wife at their rented house on Coburn Street. As the two of them bustled around the parlor, setting out benches and chairs borrowed from other rooms, he cast a fond glance at his wife. "Are you nervous?" he teased.

Maria paused in mid-flutter, noticing for the first time that she was fidgeting with the sleeves of her dress, and grinned. "I guess I am!" she confessed. "Our new mission is daring, and it hasn't seemed real until now. But now we have a departure date!"

"I know what you mean," he said, his hands on the back of the wooden chair he had just put down. "So many years of preparation, and now our plans feel oddly solid, as solid as this chair. It is strange and frightening and wonderful at the same time."

A small boy toddled through the door and wrapped one arm around Hudson's leg, the other arm busy with noisy thumb-sucking. Hudson smiled down at him. "Hello, Freddy," he said. "Did you finish all your supper?"

But the boy's eyes were fixed on the doorway.

"Apparently your son is nervous for you, too!" Maria suggested.

A pink-cheeked girl, Maria's miniature, whirled in and enticed the boy to a corner where they could take turns spinning a top. Maria's gaze followed them.

"We left China with one child," she said quietly, reaching to straighten a row of chairs, "but now Grace has three other siblings to divide our attention. She loves having the boys around, but that may change when she sees how busy we'll be."

"That is possible," he said. "Or perhaps having brothers to care for and play with will make it easier for her. She'll be less lonely and have her own role in our work."

She nodded. "I hope the burden won't be too much for the children to bear. And I am grateful that we will have Miss Bell's assistance."

A knock sounded then at the front of the house so he hurried out to answer it. Before long, the room was packed with members and friends of China Inland Mission, making their way down the short rows of chairs and chattering with excitement.

Emily Blatchley, Jennie Faulding, and Susan Barnes came in together and took seats in the front row. They and six of the other women missionaries going to China were unmarried, a reason other mission agencies had not wanted to support them. But though Hudson had been criticized for accepting them, he had stood firm. "If God has touched the heart of an unmarried woman with his passion for the perishing," he told the young women, "I will not stand in her way."

A good number of the men were unmarried, too, including tall and broad-shouldered George Duncan, short and friendly James Williamson, dramatically-mustachioed John Robert Sell, and smartly-dressed Josiah Alexander Jackson. George, towering over the room, elbowed his way along the back wall to an empty seat near his fellows.

In fact, other than the Taylors, the only married couple going to China was Lewis and Eliza Nichol. They waved hello to the others as they threaded through the packed room and slipped into the bench Jennie Faulding pointed out to them. Lewis was a blacksmith, another factor—like being single—that might keep a person from being accepted by another mission agency. Many agencies preferred well-educated candidates, people who might have more experience with foreign languages or teaching. That meant that working men like Lewis Nichol who couldn't afford to go to university usually didn't get the opportunity to become a foreign missionary—that is, unless someone with a vision like Hudson Taylor made a place for them.

So everyone in the room had a reason to respect Hudson. And when he rose to his feet, they fell quiet and gave him their attention.

"By now," he began, "you have all heard about our most recent development, the donation of our passage aboard the *Lammermuir*. I've seen the speedy clipper and she's a first-class vessel, only two years old. The captain assures me this ship can get us to China in just four months."

Excitement rippled through the room, and a man in the first row stood. "Do you trust the captain?" he asked.

"I do, Mr. Berger. He seems like a fine man. And he mentioned that at least one member of his crew is a Christian."

"And you are to leave on the 26th of May?"

"Yes. We have just a few weeks to finalize our preparations, which is why I called this meeting. I want to remind you of our principles as a mission agency, and then ask you all for a final commitment."

Everyone settled back into their chairs.

"Unlike other agencies that are directed from the home country," Hudson continued, "China Inland Mission will be directed by me on the field. I will coordinate with Mr. Berger, who will remain here to handle our home operations. I learned from my last missionary tour that when decisions are made by a home office in London or wherever, those out doing the work don't always get what they need. So the big decisions will be addressed right there in China."

"Also unlike other agencies, we will not directly appeal to our supporters for funds, but simply let Christians know about our work and trust that God will move their hearts to send us provisions. None of us is guaranteed a salary. As a team, we will see that each person has what they need, but times may be tough. We will live by faith."

He cleared his throat and went on. "As you all know, my intention is to build an inter-denominational mission. Some of you are Methodists, Anglicans, Presbyterians, Baptists. We have all agreed on the basic elements of our faith, and we have pledged to work together for the gospel without arguing over doctrinal differences. If God blesses our work and adds other missionaries to our number, we will welcome them into our family of gospel workers as well, yes?"

Heads nodded.

"I've already told you that a lot of our work will be itinerant. Though we will build a home base once we reach the interior, we will be making many trips throughout the region. Our goal is to plant churches in many locations, churches that will eventually sustain themselves. But until the native converts are able to take over, it will be our job to preach and train, and we are likely to be on the road a great deal."

He straightened his shoulders and took a deep breath. "Finally, I remind you that when we arrive, we will be leaving our English clothing behind and adopting the dress of the Chinese people. Other missionaries retain their British ways—either because they believe them superior or simply because they find them comforting in a world where so much else is foreign. But I believe the gospel will take root in China only if we are willing to celebrate the culture of the people we are there to serve. So unless a Chinese practice is sinful in itself, we should adopt Chinese ways of doing things. The Apostle Paul said he became all things to all people in order to win some of them to Christ. I intend to put his wisdom into practice in China. Is that understood?"

The group fidgeted, fingering their lace collars and bow ties.

He gave them a compassionate smile. "I know that for many of you, this will be the hardest aspect of our work. It is easy for us to become attached to our customs. But we cannot let them be a stumbling block to the gospel. Now, Mr. Nichol and I have discussed this at great length, and he disagrees with my thinking. For the time being, we are leaving the conversation open"—he gave the blacksmith and his wife a friendly nod—"but of course I hope to persuade him!"

"That about sums up our goals for this work. Anything you wish to add, Mr. Berger?" He took a step back, behind Maria's seat, and let his hand rest loosely on the curved back of her chair.

The home office director stood up again and turned to face the others. "Here in England, I will continue to publish Hudson's newsletter, so our friends here and in the States will get updates on your work. We'll also be holding regular prayer meetings for you."

"About that," said Maria, flagging Mr. Berger's attention with a lifted hand. "I intend to write many letters to Mr. Berger and other friends, and I encourage all of you to do the same. We need many praying friends!"

Mr. Berger nodded at her. "Thank you. You all have a long road ahead of you, but I am certain God will prove his care for you just as he did for Abraham, who waited on him in faith. In fact, he has already provided much of the money and supplies."

"Yes," agreed Maria, rising. "We are most excited to be taking with us the donated printing press. Since Hudson has finished his translation into the Ningpo dialect, we will be able to print and distribute Bibles as soon as we get the press set up in China."

Hudson moved to stand beside her. "My friends, we are now at a momentous occasion," he said. "Here in England, congregations of a thousand Christians worship in security while millions in China perish without knowledge of Christ. We are about to take his gospel to those millions who have never heard it before!"

The morning of their departure dawned bright, with a brisk breeze that kept the clouds scudding across the blue horizon. The missionaries gathered at the East India Docks, followed by a caravan of carts piled high with trunks, carpet bags, and packages tied with string. Their supplies would have to last the four-month voyage, plus there were all the things they would need once they got to China.

The day before, they had gathered outside the Taylors' home for a curious project. Mr. Berger had made an appointment with a traveling salesman who set up a curtained contraption on a three-legged stand. At his direction, Hudson and Maria sat down with their four children on chairs dragged out from the dining room. The other missionaries gathered around, flanking them on both sides and falling into two rows, those in the back standing behind their friends seated in front. "For posterity!" Mr. Berger had cried. The salesman ducked under the curtain and set off a bit of gunpowder, and after a brilliant flash and a puff of smoke, announced that he was finished with his unusual service. Everyone was overcome with the urge to see their images reflected on the shiny paper.

Now as they boarded the *Lammermuir*, several of the missionaries gazed fondly across the docks and wished they could just as easily light a flashbulb and burn the image of England into their mind's eyes. How long might it be before they saw their homeland again?

But Hudson didn't look back as he stepped aboard. His heart was already in China. He could feel his legs and lungs adjusting even now to the rolling tide and the salt air.

"Captain Bell," he said, spotting the skipper across deck.

"Good to see you again, Mr. Taylor," said Bell, greeting him with a mock salute. "Looks like the whole *Lammermuir* party is aboard."

"Indeed, we are. And very glad to be!"

"Excellent. I have a few tasks to attend to, but I'll find you when I have a minute to talk."

"Thank you," Hudson called, as the captain was already off again, joining crew members in an inspection of the masts.

Mr. Berger, who had assisted with the loading of their baggage, found Hudson and dabbed at his forehead with a handkerchief. "All the supplies are now aboard, my friend. Shall we gather for a farewell blessing?"

He tested a crate to be sure it would hold him, then climbed up. "Our hearts are full, O Lord," he cried, snatching off his hat and holding it over his heart.

All chattering ceased as the missionaries lowered their heads.

"Our hearts are too full for words," continued Mr. Berger, whose heart apparently still had room for words. "We have spent months praying and receiving your blessings for this trip. Though we part now, we know that if we never see each other again here on this earth, we will, according to your promises, meet again in the presence of Jesus. We pray for the preservation, spiritual prosperity, and harmony of this group and their children, as they set out to preach Christ to China's perishing millions. Bless them for the sake of your glory! Amen."

"Amen!" cried Hudson.

Conversation quickly buzzed again, the travelers hugging and wiping tears from each other's cheeks.

Hudson turned to his friend, who pulled him into a two-fisted handshake. "Our Lord will be with you the entire journey. And you, dear Mrs. Taylor," Mr. Berger said, turning to Maria, "do take care. I look forward to your letters."

She patted his arm. "I'll post the first at Anjer, if we stop there as planned. You are in my prayers."

Mr. Berger took his leave. Later, as promised, the captain came round to make sure the missionaries had secured all their belongings. "Is there anything else I can do for you?" he offered.

"Yes, there is," said Hudson. "Tomorrow is Sunday, and we plan to hold a small worship service in our cabin. But we would love to serve your crew by holding a public service on your ship, if you will allow it."

Captain Bell shrugged his shoulders. "Tomorrow may not be good, as the winds are a bit contrary. We sailors don't always get a Sabbath rest! But once we hit the open seas, it shouldn't be a problem. Plan on starting next week."

"Thank you."

"I'll even provide the saloon for you."

Hudson cocked his head. "The saloon? For worship?"

Bell grinned. "You want the men to attend, don't you? If you have it on deck, they will be in the saloon. If you have it in the saloon, they'll already be there."

"You are most gracious," Hudson said. "Know that we are praying for the safety of this ship. God willing, in four months we'll be in China."

"God willing and a strong wind, Mr. Taylor," said the captain, turning on his heel and rushing off again. "God willing and a strong wind!"

The winds started off almost too strong, forcing the crew to anchor the ship from time to time. But the band of missionaries remained cheerful. Hudson told them it was a good opportunity to get their "sea legs," and by Tuesday, when the sailing became smooth, everyone got to work. Hudson and Maria began teaching their colleagues basic Chinese vocabulary. Hudson, who had volunteered to serve as the ship's doctor, also gave lectures on medicine and surgery to missionaries and crew. Everyone helped out with chores as the captain had need, especially Mr. Nichol and the other men who were skilled at woodworking.

Hudson's band saw the ship as their first mission field. They took every interaction with the crew as an opportunity to talk about Christ. Miss Bell, the Taylor children's nursemaid, held evening Bible classes. Miss Faulding, who also helped care for the children, started reading the Bible to German crew members who wanted to learn English. Miss Degrasz did the same thing with the four Swedish crewmen. Some of the sailors showed interest. Some told them to mind their own business. And a few, including the mate, claimed to be Christians already and eagerly attended Sunday services in the saloon. As the weeks passed with chores and language classes and public worship, it seemed God was blessing them with a smooth voyage.

When they reached the Malaysian port of Anjer and dropped anchor for a day's rest and a chance to re-supply, the missionaries went ashore. Tall, rippling grasses grew in zigzags along the road, spiked with clusters of towering coconut, mango, and banana trees. As they passed a group of children around one coconut tree, a boy shimmied up the trunk and then down again just as fast, tossing the visitors a fresh-picked coconut.

Maria caught it, laughing, the liquid sloshing inside the fruit. She was surprised at the heaviness of the bark-like shell. Though she didn't speak his language, her beaming smile clearly communicated her "thank you" to the friendly child.

As they headed into the port town, they heard the pulsing beat of drums and voices raised in melody. A colorful procession came toward them, dancing and waving flags. Two men pulled carriages full of children with painted faces. "It's a wedding party!" Hudson guessed. One of the brightly-dressed men darted over to them and urged them with waving hands to come along. So they did. It was the first time they had observed a wedding performed with great jubilance in a grove of banana trees.

After the wedding, they made their way back to the town and found the local post office. They had many letters to send back to England, and to their surprise, found several letters waiting for them. Mr. Berger had sent some messages on to Anjer, hoping his friends would stop there.

Later, leaving the post office, they came upon a hotel with a café. Broad shutters filtered the tropical sun, leaving the spacious room shady and cool. Hudson and the others gathered around painted tables and ordered tea, served by Chinese waiters who were happy to help the missionaries practice their new language skills.

On the way back to the rowboats that would return them to the *Lammermuir*, Maria left the children chattering with Hudson and hung back to walk with Jennie Faulding. Maria and Jennie had become friends during these weeks on the high seas.

"This is so unspoiled," Maria said, breathing deeply of the fruited air. "What a pleasure to have a day off here—though I must admit the voyage has been easier than I expected."

"One of the best parts of the trip for me has been the opportunity to get to know your children," Jennie declared. "Grace is a precious little girl."

Maria smiled. "Thank you. Hudson tells me you had a serious conversation with her."

"Yes. I asked her some questions about Jesus to discover how much she knows about our faith."

"And?"

"Oh, I have no doubt she does, indeed, believe in Christ."

"The other day, after your conversation with her, Hudson told me that a wave broke across the deck, wetting Grace's toes," Maria recounted. "But she wasn't worried. She just said to her father, 'If the ship were to go down now, we should both be saved, should we not, papa?' Then she said she was afraid Bertie and Freddy did not love Jesus yet, and as soon as she found Bertie in our cabin, she immediately told him he must trust in Jesus."

Jennie laughed. "What a blessing your family is to all of us!"

"Ah, there is the beach again," said Maria, catching a glimpse of the turquoise water. "I suppose we must get back on the ship if we are to reach our destination."

"Let's pray it continues to be a smooth voyage!"

But the smooth part of the trip proved to be over. Shortly after they reached the China Sea, the winds rose and began to circle the *Lammermuir*, howling and pelting the ship with stinging raindrops. As Captain Bell barked orders to his crew to secure the ship, the missionaries gathered in the large main cabin to pray. But Bell soon interrupted them there, announcing, "A typhoon is upon us! Secure your personal items in the cabin to keep them from injuring anyone."

Hudson noticed blood dripping from the captain's arm. "Wait," he said, making his way to him as quickly as he could in the rocking ship. "You are injured."

The captain barely glanced at the gash. "I'll be fine."

But Hudson had already pulled a bandage from his supply and worked quickly to secure the wound. "How else can we help, Captain?"

"For now, just keep things under control down here."

He was gone again, and the missionaries scurried to tie down loose objects in all the cabins.

That night was black. Screaming winds and the violent pitching of the ship kept sleep far from everyone. Hudson felt each massive, rolling wave pushing him higher and higher into the sky where the only thing he might cling to for safety was the moon.

When morning finally arrived, the waves became gentler and the rain slackened. The missionaries rose, stiff from their sleepless night, and began to sing hymns of thanks. But the celebration did not last long. The following day, the sea became choppy again and the black clouds returned. They soon found themselves in the swirling path of another typhoon.

The winds dragged them off course. The crashing waves beat against the masts and knocked the rigging loose. The sails shredded into ribbons. The crew strained with all their might to keep the ship in one piece. But as the ocean plains became mountains, rising and falling on every side, the bow of the ship was repeatedly submerged. In the churning water, the starboard bulwarks gave way, leaving the angry waves free to race across the deck and into the cabins below. The jib-boom and the foremast broke away, and then the topmast splintered, threatening to crash through the deck. And as pieces of the ship peeled away, the sailors began to give up.

Hearing the captain shouting angrily against the storm, Hudson rushed above decks. He had noticed that since the captain's injury a few days ago, he had been growing ill. He was pale, and the muscles on one side of his face seemed to have locked up. When Hudson reached the deck and spotted Bell, he was standing at the helm in the lashing rain, gripping the wheel with shaking hands.

"But, captain! The men will be washed out to sea!" The midshipman stood at the captain's elbow, shouting to be heard above the storm.

"We will all be washed out to sea if they don't obey my orders!"

"What do you want me to do? They have barricaded themselves in the forecastle!"

"Take the helm," Bell cried, and staggered toward the forecastle, pulling his revolver from the waistband of his trousers.

But a huge wave broke over the side and swept the captain off his feet. Hudson threw himself at him, fastened a hand around his belt, and hauled him up. Bell was shivering so badly he could barely hold on to the revolver.

"Captain, violence will not help us," Hudson sputtered.

Bell shoved past him. "If these miserable sailors are afraid of dying, I'll give them the chance to get it over with!"

Another wave crested, and both men latched on to the scraps of rigging as the ship rode it down into a watery valley. For a moment, time seemed to stand still. Hudson had the sensation of lying at the bottom of a very deep bowl. Then the sides came scrolling down and the ship was climbing up again.

"Please, Captain!" he pleaded. "The passengers will help. Tell us what to do. Let me talk to the sailors!"

Bell stared at the gun in his trembling hands, slowly realizing that the gunpowder was probably too wet to fire. "All right, preacher," he sighed. "Put your people in life belts and meet me at the forecastle."

Hudson stumbled below. "Maria! Get all the women into the bowels of the ship and see if you can get the pumps working." He turned to Mr. Nichol and the other men. "Come with me. It will take every hand to save this ship!"

With the aid of the volunteers, the crew agreed to return to their stations. But even with the extra help, securing the ship seemed impossible. As soon as they fixed a line or a pump, another one broke. They bailed all night. Sunday dawned, the sun hidden behind wet, swirling clouds, and the crew and passengers worked right through their Sabbath.

Sometime during the night, the rolling of the ship seemed to subside. Hudson wondered if it was just his exhausted mind playing tricks on him. But the water level in the flooded hold seemed to be inching downward, too. And when morning came, the rain was no more than a mist hanging from a gray-washed sky. The worst of the storm was over.

Hudson put the captain to bed with medicine to fight his fever, and tended to everyone's wounds. Then the water-logged crew gathered on the battered deck to survey the damage.

When the *Lammermuir* drifted into the waters of Shanghai two days later, it was little more than a floating junkyard. Other ships that had been tucked safely in the harbor during the storm came out to see the "miracle ship." A tugboat pulled up alongside, and her captain boarded to have a closer look at the ship's condition.

"She's a mess," he declared. "It'll take months to repair her."

"That much is obvious," said Captain Bell. He had regained the color in his face and thanked Hudson for his effective doctoring—and for keeping him from a tragic mistake during the crew's mutiny.

"We'll tow you into Shanghai. You should be thankful, though. The ship we brought in last night was in the same typhoon and lost over half her crew and passengers. It's a miracle you didn't lose one!"

He marched off to set up the tow lines, and Captain Bell ordered a few men to assist him. Then he headed to the stern deck, where Hudson was gathering the passengers for a prayer service.

"Captain Bell?" Hudson prompted when he noticed him.

The captain spread his hands wide. "With the help of these nice folks in the tugboat, we will soon be landing at Shanghai."

The company broke into loud clapping.

Hudson grinned. "An old friend from my days in Ningpo lives in Shanghai now," he announced. "He has made arrangements to house us while we prepare to head into the interior. It will probably take a few weeks to arrange for transportation and gather all the necessary supplies, but it seems the longest part of our voyage is over!"

The missionaries cheered again, and Bell was happy to join them.

"It is right to give thanks to God for his salvation!" Hudson declared. "Shall we pray together?"

They all bowed their heads as he lifted his hands and prayed aloud. "Lord, you blessed us as we sought you in our feeble faith. We were at the door of eternity, but you spared us from the watery grave! And now we venture out into our next great challenge. How could we not be more devoted than ever before, seeing this evidence of your loving hand? Give us courage to take the gospel to China's perishing millions! Amen."

As soon as the tugboat got underway, everyone scurried to collect their belongings. By the time the *Lammermuir* was nudged up to the floating dock, the missionaries were more than ready to disembark. With cries of joy and great sighs of relief, they went ashore to dry land—and with them, China Inland Mission set out for the Chinese interior.

J. Hudson Taylor is known for revolutionizing the missionary movement, and the principles he pioneered are followed by most modern mission organizations. But his success came at great personal cost. The year after they arrived on the Lammermuir, *the Taylors' daughter Grace died. Three years later, Maria died giving birth to a baby boy, who lived only a few weeks. Then their son Samuel died, too. Hudson later married colleague Jennie Faulding, and they worked side-by-side for another thirty years. He died in China on June 3, 1905, at the age of 72.*

By the mid 1890s, thirty years after Hudson Taylor's return, the majority of Protestant missionaries in China were affiliated with him. Tragically, many of them were martyred in 1900 during the Boxer Rebellion, a massive violent uprising against foreigners. But the work continued, and China Inland Mission—now called OMF International—currently has more than 1,300 missionaries from 30 countries laboring to spread Christianity throughout East Asia.

Dwight Moody and Ira Sankey: What Will You Do with Christ?

OCTOBER 8, 1871. CHICAGO, ILLINOIS.

A HORSE-DRAWN CAB rolled through the streets of Chicago. It was Sunday, and the driver was grateful not to fight the businessmen and laborers that clogged the streets other days. But the closer he got to Farwell Hall, the big auditorium that was one of the city's newest landmarks, the more he had to slow down for pedestrians. Dressed in their Sunday best, they all seemed to be heading in the same direction. As he drew the horses to a halt to let a group cross the street, he noticed people clustered around a poster.

Public notices were always being nailed to fence posts and trees and around the first floor windows of the tall downtown buildings. This poster featured a sketch of a round-faced and bearded man squeezed into a black suit. Bold letters announced: "Come hear the powerful preaching of Dwight Moody and the sweet voice of the gospel singer Ira Sankey! Sundays at Farwell Hall."

The face from the poster peered out of the cab window. Removing his round black hat, he mopped the sweat from his receding hairline with a handkerchief. It wasn't a particularly warm afternoon, but the carriage was stuffy and he was dressed, as usual, in his three-piece wool suit. Replacing his hat, he pulled a pocket-watch from his straining vest and glanced at the silver face. Just in time.

The carriage stopped at the side door of Farwell Hall, and Dwight Lyman Moody climbed out. His ministry partner was waiting for him. Both men were in their thirties, but Ira Sankey was thinner and dressed more fashionably. Lambchop-style sideburns brushed his high starched collar.

"The hall's filling up, Dwight," Ira said, tipping his hat to the driver as the horses pulled away again. "Over three thousand people already! They've been arriving steadily for the last hour."

"This must be the biggest crowd so far. Seems the Lord is blessing our work, eh, brother?" Dwight took in most of the city with a sweep of his meaty hand. "This wonderful new hall, the Illinois Street church, the ministry at the YMCA. Does the 'Sweet Singer of Methodism' still think God had better work for him to do in government?"

Ira chuckled. Dwight liked to tease him about his initial resistance to joining the gospel ministry. He well remembered his first encounter with the big evangelist, just a year ago last summer.

He was on a business trip to Indianapolis. It turned out that the famous Moody would be preaching that very Sunday at a local Baptist church. Curious, Ira made his way into the already packed auditorium. He sang and played music in his spare time, so when Moody called for a song after his powerful sermon, it was natural for Ira to stand up and start a hymn. Immediately, everyone joined in.

After the service, Moody came up to him and shook his hand vigorously. "What do you do for a living, mister?"

"I work for the Internal Revenue Service. Name's Ira Sankey."

"Well, you'll have to resign, Ira Sankey. I've been looking for you for eight years!"

Ira coughed. "I beg your pardon, Mr. Moody?"

"I can preach," the big man declared, "but I can't sing. I need a voice like yours to lead the music at my gospel meetings. How soon can you come to Chicago?"

"Oh, I have a good job, sir, and a family back in Pennsylvania. But thank you for the compliment."

"How about you think about it today, and meet me out in front of the church this time tomorrow." It was a statement, not a question, and before Ira could respond the evangelist was off, handshaking his way across the congregation.

Ira was surprised at the man's confidence, but found himself strangely compelled to meet him the next day. Moody was waiting for him on the corner with a large crate.

"Climb up and start singing, Mr. Sankey."

Ira's eyebrows shot up, but again curiosity got the best of him. Shrugging, he stepped up on the crate and began to sing:

> *Am I a soldier of the cross,*
> *A follower of the Lamb?*
> *And shall I fear to own His cause,*
> *Or blush to speak His Name?*

In moments a crowd had formed around him. Ira kept singing, his smooth voice drawing passers-by who normally had to buy a concert hall ticket to hear such talented music making. As soon as he finished his song, Moody started preaching, and Ira couldn't believe the response. A half-dozen men came forward and asked Moody to lead them to Christ!

When the last businessman had thanked them and gone on his way, the evangelist said, "You see, Mr. Sankey? Come to Chicago."

It took six months and several persuasive telegrams from Moody for Ira to make up his mind. But now they had been working as a team for more than nine months, and Ira was making plans to move his family to Chicago.

"The Lord is certainly blessing our work, Dwight," he said now, dropping a hand on his friend's broad shoulder. "Though I think you give my singing too must credit. It seems no one can resist your call any more than I could!"

Inside the hall, they paused at the stage entrance to pray for the souls of everyone seated in the auditorium. Then Ira strolled out to the pump organ, and, taking his place on the bench, began to sing:

> There is a fountain filled with blood drawn from Emmanuel's veins.
> And sinners plunged beneath that flood lose all their guilty stains.
> Lose all their guilty stains, lose all their guilty stains.
> And sinners plunged beneath that flood lose all their guilty stains.

Dwight watched from the shadows at the edge of the platform as the congregation responded to Ira's music. From every corner of the room, they raised their voices to meet his:

> Dear dying Lamb, thy precious blood shall never lose its power
> 'Til all the ransomed church of God be saved, to sin no more.
> Be saved, to sin no more, be saved, to sin no more.
> 'Til all the ransomed church of God be saved, to sin no more.

The organ strains faded away. Shuffling, the crowd sat down and turned their eyes to the large pulpit and the man who filled every inch of it.

Dwight didn't wait for an introduction but plunged right into his sermon on the life of Christ. He talked about Jesus' birth, his earthly ministry, and his death and resurrection. Then he talked about the final judgment day when Jesus would return on a white horse to slay his enemies, as written in the book of Revelation.

The crowd listened intently as the preacher shouted and whispered and banged his fists on the pulpit. He was an active preacher, and an active preacher demands an active audience. They nodded, and cleared their throats, and shifted as he warned of judgment to come.

He was nearing the end of his sermon when the courthouse bells began to ring out a fire alarm. It had been a long dry season, and fires had been frequent lately. There had been one just last night, thought Dwight briefly, remembering how the alarm had roused him from sleep in the early morning. As he preached, he drew the stub of a pencil out of his vest pocket and scribbled "rain" inside the flap of his Bible. He would remember to ask for rain in his final prayer at the conclusion of the service.

"So what will you do with Christ, I ask you?" he shouted to the congregation now. "Where will you be after judgment day? Heaven? Or hell!"

He paused to let his words sink in. The people were rooted to their seats, and the only sound to be heard was the fire bell, still clanging in the distance.

"This is the most important question you will ever consider," he declared. "Think it over very carefully, and come back next Sunday with a definite answer!"

Then he turned in the pulpit to his partner at the organ. "Mr. Sankey, won't you lead us before the throne of Almighty God with one of your glorious solos?"

Ira cleared his throat and immediately began to sing:

> *Today the Savior calls:*
> *Ye Wanderers, come.*
> *Oh, ye benighted souls!*
> *Why longer roam?*

Dwight closed his eyes as Ira's voice, soft as first, became louder and more impassioned.

> *Today the Savior calls:*
> *For refuge, fly.*
> *The storm of justice falls*
> *And death is nigh!*

But now another sound was drowning out Ira's voice. A church in the next block had taken up the fire alarm bells, too, and they seemed to be growing louder and more insistent. And now they could hear people shouting in the streets. The congregation began to stream toward the exits.

Dwight and Ira, too, charged down the back stairway and out into the alley. The smell of smoke struck them like a blow. It had grown dark during the meeting, but an orange glow lit the western part of the city.

"What is this?" Ira cried.

Dwight stared at the billows of ash coming toward them across the river. "Judgment day," he whispered.

"Looks like a bad fire, Dwight. Better make sure your family is safe."

"Yes, yes," agreed the evangelist, but as Ira began to run toward the river, he called, "Wait! Where are you going?"

"To see if I can help fight the fire!"

Dwight flagged down a passing carriage. Traffic was heavy, and it took longer than usual to get to his North Side home. He flipped a coin to the driver and ran towards the front of the parsonage.

His wife met him at the door. "You're home far too early, Dwight. What's happened?"

"A fire on the South Side, Emma," he said, taking her hand. "Everything all right here?"

"Of course. But how bad is it? I mean, it's not coming this direction, is it?"

"The fire department was on their way when I left. I can't believe it would jump the river, but——."

She saw the hesitation on his face. "But what?"

"But it hasn't rained in weeks and everything is so dry. Come on, let's go inside. I'm sure it will be fine, but let's get the kids ready just in case."

His fears were realized a few hours later when, coming back from checking on the neighbors, he learned that the fire had indeed crossed the river.

"We have to go," he called to his wife, rushing back into the house. "Get Willie and little Emma and wait by the door."

She shoved their baby carriage toward him and gathered the children in her arms. He was tossing blankets, clothes, and his Bible into the baby carriage, when the front door burst open and a friend rushed in.

"Mr. Moody," he said, breathless. "The fire is heading this way. We must evacuate immediately. I have room for your family in my carriage."

Dwight pushed everyone out the door. But as he helped the children into the carriage, Emma ran back into the house.

"What—Mrs. Moody!" cried the friend, running after her. "Where are you going?"

But she ignored him. Running down the long corridor into the parlor, she yanked at a framed painting on the wall. It was a portrait of her husband.

"Mrs. Moody, please—!"

"Help me get this down," she demanded.

He was taller, and easily lifted the piece from its anchors. "You have your painting. Now, let's go!" he said, and pushed her towards the door.

They rushed back to the carriage, and Dwight pulled her inside as their friend slid onto the driver's bench and picked up the reins.

"What are you doing?" Dwight demanded, staring first at the large item in her hands and then into her distraught eyes.

His face was red with sweat. Her normally neat hair was coming out of its pins. But she clamped the frame between her feet on the carriage floor and wrapped one arm around her children and the other around her husband's moist neck. "I love this painting of you," she said simply.

And the horse lurched forward toward the outskirts of the city.

Downtown, Ira was hard at work as a link in a bucket brigade. Water sloshed over the arms of his coat as he snatched a bucket from one man and passed it in rhythm to the man on his other side. Grab a bucket, pass it. Grab a bucket, pass it. The firemen at the end of the line tossed the water on the flames, but the buckets lost a lot of their contents on their way to the fire.

Behind him, teams of horses thundered through the streets hauling steam-powered water pumpers. The city was built on Lake Michigan and had a pumping station and an impressive water tower, 154 feet high. And a system of fire hydrants had been installed recently. But most of the city was constructed with wood, and the fire was devouring it like a starving beast. A few hundred firefighters didn't seem like enough.

"Keep it moving!" cried one of the firemen, running along the line. "Keep it moving! The fire is crossing the river!"

"Music is a good motivator," Ira thought. His throat was hoarse with the stinging smoke, but he began singing a hymn at the top of his lungs.

> Shall we gather at the river
> Where bright angel feet have trod?

Grab a bucket, pass it. Grab a bucket, pass it.

> With its crystal tide forever
> Flowing by the throne of God?

Grab a bucket, pass it. Grab a bucket, pass it.

> On the margin of the river,
> Washing up its silver spray,
> We will talk and worship ever,
> All the happy golden day.

But though the buckets flew down the line, the wind was getting stronger, pushing the fire further into the heart of the city. Flames leaped higher and jumped rooftops. Black smoke rolled off the river like a deadly fog. The bridges were now thronged with people trying to get away, clutching their possessions to their chests, their screams buried under the crackling roar of the all-consuming fire.

"We're not containing it," the firemen shouted. "Forget the buckets, men! Rip out these fences—the flames are riding the pickets down the block!"

Ira began to tear at the fenceposts with his bare hands. But all around him, burning embers were raining down from the sky like huge fiery snowflakes, catching fire to the fences even as the men worked to rip them out. With a rage, the fire was overtaking the city.

And then Ira realized it was heading toward Farwell Hall. The large wooden structure was more than just a place where he and Dwight held their evangelistic meetings. It was also his temporary home while he was making arrangements to move his family to the city. Everything he had in Chicago was in that little office on the second floor.

He broke away from the fire fighters and began to run. Sparks lighted on his coat, burning brown spots into the fabric. He brushed at them with his hands as he ran, forcing his way through the crowded street to the hall.

Inside, he took the stairs two at a time. Scrambling around his office, he tossed books and clothes into a couple small trunks and shoved them down the stairs. In his haste, he kept dropping things, and whatever he picked up he just shoved into his coat pockets. It wasn't until he reached the front door, his belongings in a heap on the stoop, that he realized he couldn't carry everything. And by now it would be impossible to get a carriage.

But then a riderless horse galloped past him on the street, an empty wagon squealing behind. Ira left the trunks on the stoop and charged after the animal. But he wasn't the only one who had spotted the free ride. Fifteen men were right behind him, clawing at each other as they ran.

"He's mine!"

"No, he belongs to me. Get your own horse!"

"You're all lying! I'm the owner!"

Ira kept up for a block, until the horse skidded around a corner and the wagon rolled and fifteen men lunged for it. "There isn't enough time for this!" he sputtered. Instead, he turned back to the hall, deciding his best bet was to head toward the lake. Wrestling the largest chest onto his shoulder, he fought his way down the street toward the shore, a half mile away. The crowd thinned as he neared it, since most people were fleeing north instead. And then he noticed the site of the Palmer House hotel. It was under construction and only the cellar had been laid so far. The fire had not reached this part of the city.

He buried the chest under a pile of bricks in a corner of the cellar. Then he rushed back toward the chaos, hoping the other two trunks were still outside the hall where he had left them.

At a shelter a few miles north of the hall, Dwight and Emma made sure the children were secure in the care of their friends. It was late, and everyone urged them to stay at the shelter where it was safe. But the Moodys were worried about their neighbors. So they made their way back into the endangered area on foot, dodging carriages and banging on doors. They were shocked to find that some people had gone to bed believing that the fire was safely contained on the other side of the river.

"Wake up!" they shouted, barging into one neighbor's home after another. "The fire is coming this way! You must leave now!"

They told people where to find shelter. They urged them to take only what they could carry. They helped as many people get out as they could. But the streets were more crowded now than the Moodys had ever seen them, and they struggled just to keep from being trampled in the panic. And soon they, too, had to turn back as the marching fire sent an advance wave of ash and smoke into the North Side neighborhoods.

Later Emma and Dwight stood at a safe distance, covered with soot and trembling with exhaustion and terror. They were unable to take their eyes off the burning city. It was a dark night, and all they could see was the horrifying orange flash spreading wider and wider until it seemed even the lake must be on fire.

"It can't be possible that the whole city——." Emma stopped, then tried again. "Do you think the church——?"

Dwight slowly shook his head. "Gone," he said quietly. "Our house, too."

"Oh, Dwight! Everything we've worked for!"

He tightened his arms around her. "Everything everyone's worked for. Must be thousands of us homeless tonight. I can't imagine how many have lost their lives."

They were both quiet, running through mental lists of friends and parishioners, afraid to think of how many might already be dead. And where was Ira?

"The wisest of men are helpless tonight," Dwight said after a few minutes. "The mayor and the street sweeper are equals right now, because both have lost everything. It's like the coming day of judgment, when all will stand with naked souls before God."

They were quiet again, until Emma said, "We need to be with the children." So they turned their backs to the flames and set out in the direction of the shelter.

Downtown, Ira had stumbled back and forth through the smoke for hours. After he had deposited most of his belongings in the cellar of the hotel, he'd made the same discovery that the Moodys had on the North Shore. People living in the big houses along the lake assumed the fire was limited to the poorer neighborhoods on the South Side. But Ira, watching the flames spread faster than the water pumpers could follow, knew it was only a matter of time. So he, too, ran up and down the streets, knocking on doors and shouting warnings between coughing spasms. He couldn't believe these rich people were arguing with him about leaving their expensive homes! Finally, having warned as many people as he could, and dizzy from the smoke, he had crawled into the hotel cellar and passed out.

The sound of an explosion woke him an hour later. His head throbbed and he could barely swallow because of his thirst. A second blast roused him to his feet.

"Either the firemen are taking down strategic buildings to cut off the path of the fire," he reasoned, "or the city's gas works have been destroyed." Climbing out of the cellar, he saw that the fire was still advancing. Another boom shook the city. He realized now that the lake was his only escape.

The moon was gone, and he knew it must be nearly daybreak. The wind whipped his coat around his legs. Staggering along the water, dragging the trunks behind him, he made his way to a string of rowboats knocking against a dock. Firelight reflecting off the water revealed a man getting into one of the boats.

"Sir," Ira shouted into the wind. "Sir, are these your boats?"

"Not anymore!" the man shouted back, and was lost from sight in the rolling shadows on the rough water.

Ira hauled his trunks into the closest boat. He was desperate for water and knew it would be cleaner away from shore. He threw himself at the oars and, aided by the waves, soon put distance between himself and the dock. When he spotted pilings where a breakwater was under construction, he fumbled in the bottom of the boat for a line and tied himself to the lumber. Cupping his hands over the side of the boat, he drank until he was satisfied. Then he pulled himself up on the half-finished breakwater and looked back toward shore.

All of Chicago was aflame.

Stranded on that tiny island in the dark water, the waves thrashing the boat at his feet, Ira could think of only one thing to do. His voice was no more than a whisper through parched lips, but he sang:

> *Dark is the night, and cold the wind is blowing,*
> *Nearer and nearer comes the breakers' roar.*
> *Where shall I go, or whither fly for refuge?*
> *Hide me, my Father, till the storm is o'er.*

He dozed again and didn't wake until the sun was high above him. And still the city burned. Even out on the water, the smell of smoke reached him as the wind drove the fire right down to the shoreline. The daylight revealed wide clouds of smoke and ash stretched across the horizon.

How grateful Ira was that his wife and children were still in Pennsylvania! He had missed them the last few months, and now he was seized with a fierce desire to see them again. He thought of how many families would be grieving in the days to come, and hoped that the Moodys had escaped.

The city would be rebuilt, of course, and Ira knew he would be part of it. "I committed myself to the Lord's work in Chicago, and I'm not done," he said to himself. "But first, I'm going home to tell Fanny and the kids how much I love them!"

All he had to do now was wait out the fire. When it was safe to row back to shore, he would follow the railroad to the closest station, where he would wire a message to his wife and tell her to send him a ticket home. The nightmare would soon be over.

Two days passed before the fire finished consuming the city and finally died away. Because Dwight's ministry was well-known, the Moodys were among the first to be allowed back to survey the damage. Dwight and Emma took a carriage as far downtown as possible, until they could no longer steer the horses around the debris. Then they got out and walked.

The great city of Chicago was gone. Houses, office buildings, and churches were nothing more than heaps of blackened rubble.

Coils of burned telegraph wires snaked across the streets, the scarred paving bricks still warm under their feet. Little cyclones of ashes stirred in the breeze.

Dwight picked his way toward the site of the church. He might not have known for sure which building it was, except that he spotted on the ground the remains of a sign. He bent to pick it up. A few days ago, it had hung sharp and clean from brass hardware above the door. Now ashes darkened the blistered paint, but he could still make out the words: "Ever welcome to this House of God are strangers and the poor. The seats are free."

Dwight twisted to face his wife. "Emma, I made a terrible, terrible mistake. All those people at Farwell listening to me preach——."

"Don't even begin to blame yourself. You could not have expected the fire, and they would have lost their homes even if they hadn't come out to the hall that night."

"No, no. You don't understand. That night——." His wide shoulders sagged with regret. "I told those people to go home and make a decision for Christ by the next time we met. But how many of them never made it home that night and were lost in the fire? Why did I do that? Why did I tell them they had time? Why didn't I urge them to decide right then and there?"

Emma looked at her husband with compassion. "You were probably thinking of their safety."

"I should have been more concerned with their eternal safety!" he exclaimed, hurling the ruined sign back on the pile. "Never, never again. From this time forth I'll preach that 'now' is the only moment of salvation!"

She just nodded, waiting, respectful of the difficult lesson God was teaching her husband. Several minutes passed. Then she reached out to take his arm and said quietly, "Has anyone heard from Ira?"

He shook his head and turned back toward the road. "No one has heard from anyone. The shelters are crowded, the telegraph lines are down, there's no way to find anyone."

"I hope he's somewhere safe."

"If I were him, I'd have gone back to my family," Dwight replied. He steadied Emma as she stepped across a tangle of charred wood. "As soon as it's possible, I'll try to contact him in Pennsylvania. We're going to need his help. All I was able to save was my Bible, my family, and my reputation."

"And your portrait."

He scowled. "Oh, I'm not taking credit for that! Rescuing that silly painting was all your doing, Mrs. Moody."

"Listen, Dwight," she said, stopping in the street. "This is a tragedy of enormous proportions. But we also have reason to praise God. The whole city is in need now. We have an amazing opportunity to minister to the people of Chicago."

"You're right," he agreed. "Just think what God will do here! We have to start over, yes, but God preserved for us the same things we had when we first arrived. With the power of his Spirit, we'll do it all again."

"That's more like the confident evangelist I know," she said, pulling him toward the carriage again. "Where shall we start?"

"Perhaps a sermon at the shelter will stir people to start rebuilding the church," he replied. "There is much work to do, and we've wasted enough time already!"

The Great Chicago Fire consumed 2,600 acres and 18,000 buildings. Almost 300 people were killed and nearly 100,000 were left homeless. But out of this rubble, Moody and Sankey's ministry grew. Moody immediately put his people skills to work raising money to rebuild the church. By the time Sankey returned to Chicago two months after the fire, Moody had secured enough donations to build a temporary church. Together they organized emergency relief for those left homeless by the disaster, and their preaching and singing brought comfort and hope to many.

During the summer of 1873, the Moodys and the Sankeys traveled to the United Kingdom to preach revival. Later, Sankey became president of a music publishing company and wrote over 1,200 gospel songs. Moody returned to Massachusetts to form the Northfield Seminary for Young Women and the Hermon School for Boys. Back in Chicago, Moody's friend Emma Dryer convinced him to start a school called the Chicago Evangelization Society. It was later renamed The Moody Bible Institute, and today continues to train pastors, missionaries, and people serving God in all walks of life.

On December 22, 1899, Moody died in his home in Northfield, Massachusetts. Sankey died on August 13, 1908 in Brooklyn, New York. Chicago remains the third-largest city in the U.S. and is home to countless churches and ministries.

ROBERT THOMAS, JOHN ROSS, AND SAMUEL MOFFETT: JESUS, JESUS

SPRING 1891. MUKDEN, MANCHURIA
(PRESENT DAY SHENYANG, CHINA).

SPRING CAME DRY and cool to Mukden. The traveler was grateful for the short relief between the long, cold winter and the steaming summer soon to come. The rainy season had not begun, but melting snows rushed down from the mountains into the river basins. The irrigated fields he passed were already green, promising a bumper crop.

He paused on the road and pulled out his pocketwatch. Two hours ago, he had stood in a busy city market, watching sellers and buyers haggle over prices. Four hours ago, he had stopped at a church to introduce himself and ask directions to a village. And before that, he had wandered the streets near the docks, picking out the various dialects being spoken. Now he was on a road heading to one of the outlying villages.

He had no trouble finding the vibrantly-painted shrine at which he had been instructed to turn right. The houses in this neighborhood were small but well-kept. At the tenth house, he climbed up to the porch and called out. "Mr. Ross?"

A white-bearded man appeared in the door. "You made it, Mr. Moffett! How good to see you again." He stuck out a hand. Inky stains covered his sleeve.

The traveler gave him a firm handshake. "The pleasure is mine. It is very kind of you to offer me a bed for the night."

"We Scots take care of our own! Do come in, Mr. Moffett."

"Please, Mr. Ross, call me Samuel."

"And you're to call me John. No need for old world formalities out here, eh?" He followed his guest into the front room. "Make yourself comfortable. I'll get us some tea and let Hwa-Chung know we are ready for dinner." He disappeared through a gauzy curtain to the back of the house.

Samuel glanced around the large room, which seemed part sitting room, part dining room, and part study. It was decorated in an odd but pleasant mix of cultures. A European dining table, outfitted with the curved wooden stools found in every nearby village, anchored one side of the room. The other side was dominated by a sturdy desk topped with an ink blotter, bottles of ink, and stacks of paper.

Samuel went over for a closer look. A long scroll with Korean characters was fastened to the wall above the desk, along with several Scottish postcards. Two Bibles, one English and the other Greek, lay open on the desk.

John came back in with a tea service on a tray and set it down on the table. Samuel joined him, jerking his head back toward the desk. "I see your translation work continues," he said.

His host nodded. "We are constantly looking to improve our knowledge of the language so our translations will be more effective. Here, refresh yourself."

He accepted the cup of tea. "You seem to be making fine progress. I hope you've left some work for me! As I mentioned in my letter, I expect to do the bulk of my work in Korea."

"Plenty of work for everyone!" John gestured for his guest to take a seat at the table, and settled himself on the opposite stool.

"Though I must say it is especially nice to work with another Scottish Presbyterian."

"Aye! That's why I am hoping you will give me some direction, perhaps a bit of advice."

"Of course. I understand you've been surveying? Tell me where you have been."

"Well, most recently——."

A local boy came in with another tray. Samuel waited while the boy unloaded two steaming ceramic bowls and a pair of chopsticks for each. The sharp spice of chili peppers rose from the heap of translucent cabbage and rice. His stomach growled.

John leaned over his bowl. "Almighty God, we thank you for the work with which you have charged us and the food you have supplied to sustain us in it. We bless you for the gift of your dear son, Jesus Christ. In his name and for his sake, we pray. Amen."

"Amen."

John picked up his chopsticks. "Go on."

"Well, I'm trying to get the lay of the land, looking for the right place to set up the new mission," Samuel explained. "I've been to Pyongyang, and also looked at Uiju and that region."

He paused to slurp up cabbage with the aid of the chopsticks. The spices lit up his tongue, and immediately began to warm his chest. The food in this part of the world had been one of the first challenges to his work, but had quickly become one of his favorite perks.

"What are your impressions?"

"Well, it is vast country, and so many have not heard the gospel. I'm not sure yet where the best place is. Part of me wants to hold out for the perfect location and the right community, but another part wants to settle in anywhere so I can start focusing on preaching and teaching the catechism. This initial work seems an unfortunate delay to the real ministry."

John smiled at him. "The zeal of a young missionary. How I remember it! Though I have always been more on the literature production side of things than all the hiking and exploring your agency has you doing. Actually, you remind me of another young missionary, about your age when he set off for Korea."

"Someone I should contact? Where is he stationed? I'm bound to be in that area at some point."

"I'm afraid that's not possible," John said softly. "He's dead."

Samuel's head jerked up, sending broth dribbling down his chin. "I'm sorry," he said, blotting his face with his sleeve. "How did he die?"

"Do you know why we refer to Korea as the Hermit Kingdom?"

"Of course. The king insists on a foreign policy that excludes Westerners."

"Yes. The closer our work appears to assist that of Western statesmen and militaries, the harder it is for us to bring the gospel. The fact is, when Koreans become convinced of the gospel, they become the best missionaries to their own people. That's why I want to produce the best possible Korean Bible translation and then get the national converts to take it back to their villages and teach it."

"But what about this young man who died?"

"His is a tragic story." John paused, looking into his bowl. "His name was Robert Jermain Thomas. Welsh by origin and Church of England by creed. Fearless, it seems."

"Robert Thomas," Samuel said thoughtfully. "I think I've heard his name before."

John nodded. "His story is already something of a legend. He came to Korea, as did I, through the encouragement of a dear friend—another Scotsmen, I might add—Alexander Williamson." He smiled sadly. "Unfortunately, the good Mr. Williamson also died recently. I have now taken over his work."

He fortified himself with another bite, and swallowed before continuing. "Anyway, Robert graduated from New College in Edinburgh around '62 or '63, I think. He was immediately ordained, and married a young woman by the name of Caroline. Wedded only a few months, the couple were sent to Shanghai by the London Missionary Society. But things were tough from the start, and while Robert was in another city, she died."

"How sad!"

"As you can imagine, he was terribly distraught. And the missionary society rejected his request to serve somewhere else—he felt there were plenty of missionaries in Shanghai, compared to the many unreached areas—so he resigned his commission in '65. Decided to go it alone. Went to Chefoo. That's where he met Williamson."

Samuel pushed away his empty bowl and leaned forward on his elbows. "Williamson was working with the National Bible Society of Scotland, like you are now?"

"Yes. Williamson told him Catholic missionaries had penetrated the closed Korean border. He and the Bible Society were trying to get Bibles and other books to the Catholic converts, but it was a stealthy business. The mere possession of Christian materials in Korea could result in death. Well, Robert had no wife now and no agency to report to, so he volunteered to smuggle in a supply of Bibles. Two escaped Korean converts went as his guides, and they spent three months visiting secret congregations and handing out Bibles. He returned to Williamson with renewed zeal. But then…"

"Let me guess. Persecution?"

"That seems to be the cycle of things." John put his bowl to his lips and drank the last of the broth. "Several French priests escaped into Chefoo, reporting that Catholics were being massacred. Robert was desperate to go back and encourage the survivors. To gain entry, he agreed to go along on a French expedition intended to negotiate for the safety of their priests. But the expedition got cancelled."

"What did he do then?"

John sighed. "He found another way in. And that's where his story takes a second tragic turn."

~ ⋄ ~

The harbor smelled of sulfur and the sweat of dockworkers moving cargo. For two days, Robert had paced the harbor district, sizing up boats and going into the shipping offices to find out where they were headed. He hadn't really expected any of them to go straight into Korea, but he hoped to go at least part of the way by water. So he was surprised to discover that one ship intended to sail all the way to Pyongyang. He stood on the pier and looked it over carefully.

The *General Sherman* was registered in the shipping office as an American schooner. The red, white, and blue flag flying at the bow confirmed it. Sails flanked a central smokestack, and cannons protruded from the iron hull, pockmarked by battle. But it was clearly seaworthy. And the dockworkers were loading crate after crate of some kind of merchandise, which made Robert curious. If they were going to Pyongyang, why were they taking so much cargo? The Hermit Kingdom did not trade with Westerners.

"Excuse me!" he shouted to the crew. He glanced at the note the shipping clerk had given him. "Excuse me! May I speak with Captain Page or Mr. Preston, please?"

"Who's asking?" came the distracted reply.

"A man with a proposal for your superiors."

A deckhand frowned down at him and grumbled, but disappeared across the deck. Several minutes later, another man appeared. Lean and muscular, he crossed the bowing gangplank with sure steps. "I'm Captain Page. What can I do for you, Mr.——?"

"Robert Thomas." The young man stuck out his hand and offered a firm handshake.

"What can I do for you, Mr. Thomas? As you can see, we're rather busy here."

"I'm looking for passage into the Korean interior, and I understand you're about to set out in that direction."

The captain folded his arms across his chest. "This isn't a passenger ship, Mr. Thomas."

"I can see that. But surely you have room for just one?"

"And what price do you offer for your passage?"

"I have no money. But I've spent a few months in Korea, and I could serve as your translator. No point in doing business with people if you don't know the language well enough to negotiate prices, right?"

"And how do I know you're good enough with the language?"

"I was to translate for the French Admiral Roze on an official government expedition into Korea. Unfortunately, it has been postponed. That's why I came to you. I need to get as far up the Taedong River as possible."

Page's eyes narrowed. "Why? What's your business there?"

Robert decided it was only fair that the captain know what he was getting into by taking him on as a passenger. "I'm a missionary," he admitted. "It's against Korean law to be a Christian, but many Koreans have decided to do it anyway, and I'm trying to support them. I've got a few crates of Bibles and I intend to smuggle them as deep in the interior as I can get."

"Bit of a rogue, then, aren't you? You might have said that first off."

"You never know who you can trust."

At this, the captain burst into laughter. "All right, Thomas. Didn't think I'd welcome a 'holy man' to my crew, but we could use your services. Translation services, that is—there'll be no preaching to my men. Understood?"

"Yes, captain. Thank you. If I have my Bibles delivered to the dock—?"

Page waved off the question. "Yes, yes, we'll get them loaded up." He sprinted back up the gangplank, then turned back. "Be aboard by 5:00 tonight. We sail as soon as we get clearance!"

Robert went back to Williamson's house and hired a rickshaw driver to deliver the crated Bibles to the dock. It took only minutes to pack up the few belongings he would need, so he spent the rest of the afternoon saying good-bye to his friends. By early evening, he was on the deck of the ship being introduced to the crew.

Captain Page had another man with him, a bit shorter than the captain and thicker around the middle. "Mr. Thomas, this here is Mr. Preston. He owns this ship. We'll be leaving port soon, so you'll have to excuse me. I expect the two of you want to talk."

"Welcome aboard, Mr. Thomas," said Preston, offering his hand.

"It's a pleasure to meet you. Quite the ship you have here."

"She's my pride and joy. Come along and I'll introduce you to her." He began to cross the deck toward the smokestack, and Robert matched his pace. "The *General Sherman* is a retired U.S. gunboat that served in the Civil War. You said you're from Wales? Well, she's from Scotland—built in '61 in Glasgow—so a fellow European for you! Anyway, she's 198 feet 9 inches by 27 feet 3 inches by 16 feet. As you can see, she runs on both steam and sails, and is armed with several cannons."

He was beaming like a proud father, so Robert said, "Impressive."

"Yes, she is, and Page is a strong captain. The crew takes good care of her."

Robert glanced around the deck at the men readying to cast off. "Looks like it's a rather mixed crew."

Preston nodded. "Page and I are Americans, obviously, but Mr. Hogarth over there is English. Most of the sailors are Chinese. We'll be picking up a Chinese pilot when we get to the mouth of the Taedong. We'll need his experience for a voyage like this."

"Do you really intend to sell goods in Pyongyang? It's hard to believe the government has changed its policy on foreign trade."

"I have a load of cotton goods, tin sheets, and glass that I'm betting will change their minds," he said with a grin.

Robert cocked his head and squinted at him. "So you don't have special permission, then?"

"From what Page tells me about you, I have as much 'special permission' to ply my trade there as you have to ply yours."

Robert didn't reply. His situation was clearly different, but how could he explain that to this businessman?

"Look," Preston continued. "The Koreans need goods, and I have goods to sell them. The king can't keep a whole country shut off from the world! So I'll force the issue a bit, and if there's trouble, well, we're armed." He shrugged. "I recommend you arm yourself as well. At least to help protect the ship."

Robert's heart leaped in alarm. What kind of men were these merchants? He said, "I own a pistol and a sword, but I've never used them on a man."

"Some men do not leave you a choice." Preston gestured for him to follow. "Now let me show you the rest of the ship."

Robert was quiet for the rest of the tour. He couldn't help but notice that every crewman was armed. They seemed friendly enough, but doubt nagged at him. Was a gunboat really the best way for a missionary with a message of peace to get up the river? But what other option did he have? Few ships would take the risk of sailing in without an invitation by the king. It might be months before he found another way to get in.

No, this is it, he decided. God had provided transportation, and he would take it. He would also be careful and pray a lot. If things got unpleasant, he could always leave the ship and go on foot. At least he would have saved himself some time. How he wished he could have talked this over with Caroline! She had a good instinct about people. But he couldn't dwell on sad memories now. He had work to do, and finally he was getting the opportunity to do it.

Preston went below, but Robert stayed above, thinking through his plan as he waited. The steam engines began to rumble, and soon he felt the jolt as the *General Sherman* left the dock.

Within the week, they had entered the Taedong River. As Preston had informed him, they stopped at the port on the mouth of the river to pick up another crew member and a few more supplies. It was a wide river, and deep, though the pilot warned that the water level was lower than usual. So they sent ahead a blue boat to keep testing the depth. Running aground would not be advantageous for trade.

They cast anchor near the first sizable village. Robert went with Preston in the blue boat to the small dock, where a crowd had gathered at the appearance of the ship. Preston was overjoyed that several local merchants agreed to board the ship to look over his merchandise. Robert translated as they negotiated prices, and rode back to shore with them so he could pass out a few Bibles. It was a quiet start to his work, and he went to sleep in his bunk that night praying the rest of it went just as quietly.

The crowd was bigger at the next stop. As Robert talked to the people, he learned that word had spread from the previous village that the odd-looking ship carrying curious treasures was heading up the river. He took the opportunity to speak of Jesus, and was surprised when a wrinkled old woman began to cry.

She drew close and furtively pulled out a string of prayer beads with a crucifix from under her shirt. "Our priest was executed and all our holy books taken! Please, do you have more?"

"This is why I have come!" he told her, trying to contain his excitement. "Can you help me distribute these?"

"I'll hide them and tell the other believers where to find them. Oh, they'll kill us if we are caught with them! But we have no one to teach us now and must do what we can. God bless you!"

The blue boat went back and forth to the ship all day, Robert praying with the local Christians in between translating. When he finally got aboard for the night, Preston was grinning.

"Fantastic work, my friend," he said, slapping his translator on the back. "Your preaching is bringing more people to this ship than we expected. You are more of a curiosity than my goods! Hermit Kingdom no more."

But later as the ship moved up the river again, Robert noticed a number of small boats stationed at intervals along the shore. He had a feeling they were local officials.

The following day, they dropped anchor at the next bend of the river. He again took the blue boat to shore, inviting traders out to see the merchandise and then preaching to any who gathered. He'd been busy for hours when the crowd parted to make way for a small squadron of men armed with long daggers. Robert recognized them as the local police force.

The commander came over to Robert and asked if he spoke Korean. When Robert said yes, he continued, "I'm an officer of the governor of Pyongyang Province, who requests that you declare your purpose for sailing the Taedong. What is your business here?"

Robert decided it was better to leave Preston and Page out of it. "I am a religious emissary, a Christian missionary," he explained.

"All foreign religions are forbidden by the king," the officer replied. "Christians not allowed."

"Oh, yes," said Robert, thinking quickly. "I understand the Catholic priests have been, uh, outlawed here. But I'm not Catholic. I'm Protestant, a different kind of Christian."

"You are delivering literature and meeting with the followers of these priests?"

"I may have, but technically we hold to certain different doctrines——."

"Christian is Christian, and it is forbidden," the officer interrupted. "You are unwise to bring a ship full of outlawed teachers up the river."

"No, no, I'm the only Christian. The other men are peaceful traders. They simply wish to open trade in this territory."

"Trade is also forbidden by the king. The governor has no authority to change that. You must turn back. The governor wants no trouble in his province."

Robert cleared his throat. "I understand. Well, I will take this message back to the captain," he promised.

The officers waited as he boarded the blue boat and headed back to the *General Sherman*. As he climbed aboard, he saw they were still standing at the dock, watching.

Preston demanded to know what they had said. When Robert told him, he shook his head violently. "Nonsense. We're making no trouble for anyone, just selling things to people who want to buy them. We keep moving up the river toward Pyongyang."

So instead of turning the ship around, they ran up the sails and moved forward. The blue boat kept testing the water depth, but the next day as they approached the Crow Rapids, where the water levels varied, they ran aground. The ship hit the sandbar with a shudder, and listed to one side.

Robert was not surprised when a police boat approached that afternoon with a message. It was from the governor, warning them to go no further and to turn back as soon as they were free from the sandbar. Robert wondered if he should turn back, maybe take as many Bibles as he could carry and set out on foot.

A storm blew in before nightfall, and for hours, heavy rains drummed on the iron hull. He couldn't sleep, so he was awake to feel the ship shifting in the riverbed. He ran above decks to see that the tide was coming in and the river swelling with rainwater. By mid-morning, the ship had righted itself. But instead of turning around and heading back to China, Preston gave the order to sail on.

Within a few days, they were in sight of Pyongyang, the capital city. And as soon as they anchored, the governor again sent out a boat to deliver a message. This time, Robert and the *General Sherman's* mate went out in the blue boat with a few members of the crew to meet them.

As he faced the other boat, Robert thought the Korean police captain looked about his own age. He briefly wondered if he was married and if he would find Wales as strange and exciting as Korea was to him. But the young man had wasted no time and was delivering his message in rapid Korean.

"What is he saying?" asked the mate.

"He's warning us to turn back," Robert translated. "For all they know, we work for the French, whose priests were killed recently, and we're scouts for an invasion fleet to come later. Or they think we might be another band of Chinese pirates come to ravage their shores again."

"Chinese pirates!"

Robert faced the mate squarely. "Half your crew are Chinese. Apparently they get invaded by pirates quite often along this shore. You can understand why they are suspicious."

The mate pushed him back to face the Korean boat. "This is ridiculous! Just tell him we're here to trade, that's all."

Robert spoke with the captain again, but his response was the same. "He says we must turn back or face serious consequences. The government is officially warning us."

"He needs to tell that directly to Captain Page and Mr. Preston," said the mate.

Robert communicated that to the Korean captain, but the young man shook his head. "He says he does not have permission to board our ship and that it would be unwise," he translated again. "He says all we need to know is that we are to leave immediately."

"He can explain that face-to-face to Captain Page." The mate gestured to his two crewmen, and they reached out and latched onto the side of the police captain's boat.

The Korean officers grabbed at the rocking boat to steady it, and by the time they had reached for their daggers, the mate's crewmen had pulled revolvers.

The police captain argued, his face flushed, and Robert translated as fast as he could. But the mate refused to listen and Robert turned on him in frustration. "Are you trying to get us killed?" he shouted.

"You are free to leave anytime," the mate insisted. "But I can't vouch for your safety on land." He pointed toward shore, where several Korean officers had been watching the encounter and began to spread out along the water's edge.

Robert sat down heavily as the blue boat dragged the other boat toward the *General Sherman*. When they docked, the two Korean officers jumped off and swam toward shore, but the captain defiantly let the mate lead him aboard. Preston and Page were waiting.

"Who are you?" Preston demanded

"He's the police captain," Robert said angrily. "Your crew just kidnapped him!"

A new sound carried over the water, and the men turned to face the shore. A crowd was gathering, and they were shouting.

"Mr. Preston," Robert said, turning to him, "I'd say the locals are not happy tin and cotton buyers anymore. They're demanding you let their officer go."

Preston ignored him. "How do I know you represent the Korean government?" he said to his captive.

Robert threw his hands in the air and translated the question for the police captain. The Korean kept his stare on Preston while he reached into his uniform and pulled out a document bearing the government seal.

The shouting from shore was growing louder. Preston frowned. "We can't talk out here. Take him below."

"That would be unwise," Robert insisted. "You'll just make the people more angry."

"Your job is to translate, Mr. Thomas, not to give orders!" Preston stomped across the deck, his crew following with their hostage.

Robert slumped to his knees in despair. How had it come to this? If Caroline hadn't died or if the Korean king hadn't executed the Catholic priests or if he had just stayed in Wales in the first place! All he wanted to do was deliver the gospel. Now he was an accomplice in an international hostage situation!

That night, Preston, Page, and the mate sat up arguing in the captain's quarters. Robert didn't bother to join them. He wanted nothing to do with them at this point, but leaving the ship with an angry crowd on shore was too risky. "Which means I'm a hostage now, too," he realized bitterly.

In the morning, the governor himself rowed out to the ship to demand the release of his police captain. But still, Preston and Page refused. They had decided that if they released their prisoner, the locals would attack, but as long as he was on board, the governor would hold them off. Once they had safely escaped, they could set him free.

So they took up anchor and pulled forward again. When the locals saw the foreign ship begin to move, taking their policeman with it, they loosed a volley of flaming arrows.

Robert was in his bunk when a thunderous blast knocked him to the floor. "Cannon?" he exclaimed. He scrambled up, belted on his revolver, and ran up the stairs. "What are you doing?" he shouted at Captain Page when he reached the deck.

"They're attacking us with their pitiful arrows!" the captain spat back. "We are firing our cannons above their heads as a warning."

"A warning! Where do you think those cannonballs are going to land?"

"Captain," the mate yelled, running up. "We can't send out the blue boat. It's too exposed and the men will get hurt."

"Then let's hope the water stays deep enough!"

They dashed off to secure the smaller boat, leaving Robert standing there with his mouth open. Another wave of burning arrows sent him scurrying for cover.

And the next day, a grinding metallic crunch announced that the ship had run aground again. But this time, it was followed by a terrible cheer from the direction of the shore. Robert saw that the crowd had followed them along the river, and now that the ship was stuck, began to attack them with arrows again. One of the crewmen was hit in the neck, and plunged overboard.

"Man the cannons!" Page shouted.

The grounded ship rumbled with the blast of cannons. Robert watched helplessly as Korean boats began to row toward them, shoving ahead flaming wooden rafts piled with salt. Thick, yellow smoke enveloped the deck. The crew began to blindly fire their revolvers over the side.

Eyes stinging, Robert dashed to the cargo hold and pried open a crate of Bibles. He scooped up as many as he could carry and forced his way back up to the deck again. A shot rang out, and a bullet tore into the mast just above his head.

He started throwing Bibles into the oncoming boats, shouting, "Jesus, Jesus!" Choking on smoke, he finally leaped over the side of the ship into the water, trying to keep the Bibles above his head. He was soon wading toward the writhing crowd shrieking at water's edge. Fist-sized rocks battered his face and chest.

"Jesus!" he kept sputtering, waving the Bibles. Blood poured from his nose, and as he bent to wipe it on his shirt, he saw the revolver still strapped to his hip. "No, I'm not your enemy!" he cried, trying to remember the Korean words. "I'm here to tell you about Jesus. Jesus!" He began to throw the Bibles to them.

Then he stumbled at the edge of the water and sat down with a splash. A police officer shoved the crowd back, looming over him. Head spinning, Robert tried to fix his gaze on the young man's eyes. He held out the last Bible to him. "Jesus," he gasped again.

The officer looked at the book, at Robert's bloodshot eyes, and then back at the book. Finally, he took the Bible in one hand while he raised his sword with the other.

John Ross paused in his account. The quiet hung like a fog in the room, so heavy that the squeak of Samuel's chair as he leaned forward startled them both.

"Well, that's it?" Samuel demanded. "I mean, what happened to him?"

"Some say the officer beheaded him right then and there. Others say he was beaten to death by the crowd. The Koreans have two or three versions of what happened, and the Americans have their own, too." John shrugged. "That's the best account I can put together. In the end, it doesn't really matter how he died. The fact is that when the smoke finally cleared, the entire crew of the *General Sherman*, including Robert Thomas, was dead."

"What a loss," Samuel groaned, slumping back on the stool.

"It seems a feeble beginning to the gospel here, I know. But, Samuel, a beginning is all we needed!"

"Of course. But—might not there have been a better way?"

"I won't pretend to have God's point of view. I know that humans always make mistakes. But I also know that Robert and the French Catholics who took such risks made our current work possible. We have their persistence to thank for Korea starting to open up."

Samuel sighed. "Indeed, and I praise God for his sovereignty. But how sad for Mr. Thomas."

They were silent again. Then John said, "So what will you do now?"

Samuel turned his attention back to his companion. "Tomorrow I'll continue on my journey. I need to visit a few more locations before the agency decides which one is more strategic. But wherever we decide, I'll start preaching and holding catechism classes. The agency has promised to send several medical missionaries to join me there."

"I'll be praying for your great success! And you'll let me know how I can assist? Well, I'm sure you're quite tired and I'm happy to say Hwa-Chung has fixed a very comfortable bed for you tonight. Perhaps you'd like to retire?"

"Aye, thank you. It has been a long day."

They rose, and Samuel picked up his bag to follow his host. But John turned back to him suddenly. "You know, I wouldn't be surprised if some of your future catechumens are still using Bibles Robert Thomas carried in."

"Wouldn't that be something?"

John nodded and turned toward the door again. "Anyhow, let me show you to your room."

The bed was comfortable and Samuel was exhausted. But he found it took him longer than usual to fall asleep. His mind kept turning over Robert Thomas's tragic ministry and wondering just what really had happened on that river.

After a few days in Manchuria, Samuel set out for the jungle again. He made several survey trips over the next year. In Uiju, a man named Han Suk-Chin became a Christian in response to Samuel's preaching, and committed himself to working with Samuel and the other missionaries. When they decided to build the mission in Pyongyang, it was Suk-Chin who purchased land on West Gate Street. And it was Suk-Chin who discovered the great surprise.

"There you are," Suk-Chin called, entering the mission's kitchen one morning. Samuel was eating breakfast, as usual with a book in his hand.

"Oh, good morning, Suk-Chin. Any word on when the medicine will arrive?"

"Not yet. But I have other news. Remember how you asked me about a Welshman and some Chinese Bibles?"

Samuel looked up in surprise, the pages flipping rapidly as he set down the book. For two years, he had been unable to forget the story John Ross had told him. It had been on his mind the second time he had visited Pyongyang, before he bought the mission station, but either no one there knew about Robert Thomas or they had been afraid to admit it. Later, he had asked Suk-Chin if he'd heard of the incident, but he was from Uiju and only knew a few more people in Pyongyang than Samuel.

"I thought you'd forgotten about that," Samuel said.

"No, tragic story!" Suk-Chin shook his head. "But I think you want to see what I found."

Samuel scrambled to his feet. "Someone who knew Mr. Thomas?"

"Come see."

He left his breakfast and his book, and followed his colleague out of the mission. They turned left off West Gate Street, and headed south. After twenty minutes of walking, he said, "Suk-Chin, tell me where we're going! I don't even have my hat."

"Almost there."

Ten minutes later, Suk-Chin stopped in front of a house. It was one of several tucked into the trees, and looked old. But with the hard rains and the ever-encroaching jungle, it wasn't always easy to tell how long a building had been standing, or if it was inhabited.

"What is this place?" asked Samuel.

"You said the man who killed Thomas took a Bible from him, yes?"

He shrugged. "That's what I was told. But there are a lot of missing details."

Suk-Chin pointed. "This was his house."

"You mean the officer's?" Samuel's eyes widened. "This was his house?"

"Come inside. You see."

Samuel nearly walked on Suk-Chin's heels as he followed him inside. It was dim and musty. The first room was empty, except for an old man sitting on the floor, apparently dozing.

"Is that the man?" he whispered.

"No. He just keeps watch from time to time. Keeps the place clean for visitors."

Samuel glanced at the filthy floor, but didn't comment. "What visitors?"

"They come to see." Suk-Chin dropped a coin in the lap of the old man, who suddenly scooted aside and produced a lantern from the corner behind him.

They left him and went through a doorway to the back of the house. It was divided into two rooms, and Suk-Chin led the way to the far one. He lit the lantern and handed it to Samuel.

The missionary's mouth dropped open as he hoisted the lantern, casting an arc of yellow light across the room. The walls were covered with uniform pieces of paper, the size of a book. In fact, they might have been pages torn from a book. A book with very thin pages and covered with Chinese characters about a man walking on water and calming a sea.

"A Bible?" Samuel cried. He put his fingertips on the page directly in front of him. Like the others, it was tattered and moldering.

"The old servant says this was the guest room of the Welshman's executioner," Suk-Chin explained. "That he brought home the Bible he got from the Welshman, tore it apart, and decorated the walls with it because it was exotic and he wanted to impress his friends. And that as he saw it every day he became interested in the stories and came to believe in the God it described. And many of his friends did, too. They read and then became Christians."

Samuel stared at him, stunned. "This has been here all this time, so close to us?"

"It was kept secret for many years. Even now, few people know. But the old man and some others take care of the place. It has become like a shrine to people who remember the old days of fear."

Samuel shook his head and laughed, quietly, because the room felt holy with those words on the wall. "John Ross was right. I thought his ministry was cut short, but Robert Thomas has been preaching Jesus all these years! From this house!"

His colleague shrugged. "Like his savior, his work lives on."

"Amen," Samuel agreed, clapping his companion on the shoulder. "What a blessed reminder! Come, let's go back to the mission. I have to write someone about this!"

***

Thousands of Catholic missionaries and converts were executed during the year before the "General Sherman incident," when Robert Thomas joined them as the first Protestant martyr. He was 27. This first international conflict in Korea set the tone for many others, spilling a lot more blood.

But Thomas's martyrdom and John Ross's translation work did pave the way for Protestant missions in Korea. Encouraged by their efforts, Samuel A. Moffett started a preaching ministry that was heavily influenced by Dwight Moody. He was eventually joined by other men and women missionaries, many of whom were doctors and teachers. He helped found Union Christian College (now called Soong Jun University) and Presbyterian Theological Seminary (now Presbyterian College and Seminary) in Seoul, South Korea. Today, nearly 10 million Koreans call themselves Christians, and Seoul is home to the largest Presbyterian congregation worldwide. Other than the United States, South Korea sends out more foreign missionaries than any other country.

Religious persecution still abounds in North Korea, however, where hundreds of thousands of Christians currently suffer in communist concentration camps.

LIVING THE GOLDEN RULE

THE GOSPEL OF Matthew records Jesus teaching his disciples a lot about loving their neighbors and doing good for others. In Matthew 7:12, Jesus put his teaching this way: "Whatever you wish that others would do to you, do also to them." This statement has often been called the *Golden Rule*, because it is a simple (though sometimes hard to practice!) way to live in harmony with other people.

As the world has gone through great upheaval over the last two centuries—inventing, building, discovering new challenges and trying to overcome them—Christians have been mindful of Jesus' teachings. Trying to live out the Golden Rule has led to them being at the forefront of change, encouraging their churches, communities, and governments to take actions that would better the lives of their fellow human beings. Often this takes the form of discussions about people's "rights."

In earlier centuries, Christians emphasized the individual's duty to serve the lord of the land or the master of the household.

There was very little room for the rights of individuals. But as *democracy*—rule by and for the people—rose up in some parts of the world, the rights of individuals came into greater focus and required Christians to think carefully about what these should look like, given the Golden Rule.

Rights are sometimes understood in categories, such as *human rights*, those rights granted by God (like the right of each person to life) and *civil rights*, those rights granted by government (like the right to vote or own property). But human rights cannot be protected without the existence of civil rights—the two work together. So Christians have played various roles in securing these rights for themselves and for others.

HUMAN RIGHTS

In England, near the beginning of the nineteenth-century, Christians like William Wilberforce made public the plight of human beings sold into slavery. He told England and the world they were obligated to pursue a "great change" that would end the slave trade and recognize the human rights of precious people made in God's image. In 1807, the British Parliament passed the *Abolition of the Slave Trade Act*, and in 1833, existing slaves were legally freed.

Around the same time, this charge was being sounded in America, where some northern states, like New York, were leading the way in freeing slaves. But securing freedom for all was a struggle in a country where southern cotton and tobacco plantations relied on slave labor. The rights of states to pass their own slavery laws became a constant debate and was one of several big issues leading to the start of the *American Civil War* in 1861. Christians stood on both sides of the war, arguing either for their rights to own slaves or for the rights of slaves to be free, and these arguments were often the themes of Sunday sermons. But President Lincoln issued the *Emancipation Proclamation* in 1862 and 1863, and after the war ended in 1865, the *Thirteenth Amendment* of the U.S. Constitution finally ended the slavery system in that country.

In India, the campaign for human rights was led by figures such as Pandita Ramabai, a highly-educated Christian teacher. Her focus was on the terrible treatment of young widows. Indian men often married very young girls, and when the husbands died, their child widows were sent away for the rest of their lives—or worse. The common practice of *sati* encouraged a young widow, seen as her husband's property, to be burned alive on the funeral pyre with her husband's body. Ramabai called India to recognize the human rights of these women, and in the meantime gave her life to rescuing these women and providing them with loving care and education so they could minister to others.

In Germany, Lutheran pastor and theology professor Dietrich Bonhoeffer fought for the rights of Jews during World War II. Many churches in Germany overlooked Hitler's death camps in favor of patriotism. But Bonhoeffer believed that Christians must recognize the value of all human life and withstand dictators like Hitler, so he helped Jews escape from Germany and joined a resistance movement.

In Uganda in the 1970s, Janani Luwum was an Anglican archbishop. He believed it was his Christian duty to call Uganda's "President for Life," Idi Amin, to repent of his murderous rampages against his own countrymen assumed to be his enemy.

And in Hawai'i, Princess Ka'iulani saw her people losing their freedom to rule themselves at the hands of cunning American businessmen and politicians who wanted to *annex* (claim as their own) her nation. The men who had orchestrated the takeover were professing Christians, the grandsons of missionaries who had come to the islands decades earlier. But the 17-year-old crown princess came to America to remind the president and the U.S. Congress that Christian principles of morality and integrity were being ignored, and she pleaded with them to return her country to the native people.

The fight for the basic human rights of those made in God's image continues throughout the world. In many instances, Christians are leading the charge. Organizations like *International Justice Mission* work to free the 27 million slaves remaining in the world today. And *Compassion International* and *World Vision* are just two of numerous Christian relief organizations fighting world hunger and malaria and offering aid to genocide victims in Darfur and elsewhere.

CIVIL RIGHTS

Civil rights force human beings to recognize the essential human rights of others. The absence of civil rights is a pretty good indicator that a society considers some people of less value than others. For example, *suffrage*, or the right to vote, was in many countries not available to all the people who lived there.

For centuries, voting rights were limited to white males in many parts of the world. In America, the rights of black men to vote weren't established until 1870, and the rights of women (black or white) to vote came even later, in 1920. Voting rights for women came later in many other countries, too, including Germany (1918), England (1928), France (1945), and India (1950). Some Christians opposed voting rights for everyone but white males. Based on Scripture, they argued that slaves are to be subject to their masters and wives to their husbands, so none of those people should be allowed to vote. But other Christians saw it differently, believing the Bible teaches that all people are created equally. Former slave Amanda Berry Smith (1837-1915), for example, who was both black and female, read Galatians 3:28 as her Christian duty to call others to Christian equality, and she became a leading voice in the American suffrage movement.

It is no surprise, then, that the American *Civil Rights Movement* during the 1960s reflected the connection between human and civil rights. Reverend Dr. Martin Luther King, Jr., a Baptist minister, fought for the rights of black men and women in America, who were still discriminated against even though they had won the right to vote. During the years of that movement, black Americans frequently suffered violent hatred, like when four little girls in Birmingham, Alabama, were murdered when a bomb was detonated at the 16th Street Church during morning worship. It was Reverend King's dream that "one day this nation will rise up and live out the true meaning of its creed: 'We hold these truths to be self-evident, that all men are created equal.'" Some white Christians joined their black brothers and sisters in civil rights demonstrations to proclaim their love and support.

Today, Christians often disagree about how to fight injustice and promote human rights. Some believe in political action, and others believe in private and personal action only. Some work through the local church, and some work through non-church organizations. But however they do it, they seek to live out the Golden Rule as they resist with the gospel the effects of sin, and actively love their neighbors.

Pandita Ramabai: Miseries into Sweetnesses

SUMMER 1892. PUNE, MAHARASHTRA, INDIA.

ONE BY ONE, the girls completed their evening chores and slipped out to their teacher's sitting porch. Beyond the stone columns, distant mountains faded into twilight, their reflections on the river dissolving into shapeless purple ripples. On both sides of the water, lamps flared like fireflies as the residents of Pune gathered on neighbors' porches with their pipes and needlework, ready to take advantage of the cooler air.

Claiming their usual places on the carpet, the students greeted each other quietly. Conversation was all whispers—except for Manoramabai. She chattered away while she turned up the oil lamps, the warm glow animating her rounded features.

"I wish you had been there. I wish all of you had been there!" she was saying. "Your mothers would have given their best saris to hear her speech, I promise. No woman had ever spoken to the National Social Congress before, and here she was telling them they were all wrong about how they treat women!"

"Mano," interrupted one of the older girls. "You are always telling this story. But you were only seven or eight when it happened. Do you even remember it properly?"

Manoramabai's large eyes flashed in the lamplight. "No one there has forgotten that moment!" she insisted. She turned toward the darkening river, shook out her hair dramatically, and settled one delicate hand at her throat. "'Don't be surprised that my voice is small, countrymen—for you have never given a woman a chance to make her voice strong!' She said it, just like that, Mother did. And then she kept right on going, giving the delegates a severe talking to, and they sat there and listened to every word!"

"Manoramabai." The voice that had spoken so strongly to the congress came now from the arched doorway, just as firm but warm with affection.

The girl scrambled to her place on the carpet. If there was one thing that made her mother uncomfortable, it was people talking about her good deeds. Especially Mano, who was supposed to be learning to prize humility and servanthood above all other gifts.

The woman barely made a sound as her bare feet crossed the carpet. She joined the circle of girls, sitting cross-legged on the rug and sweeping the hem of her white cotton sari beneath her. She was short and small-boned, and she looked almost childlike as she sat perfectly still for a moment, head bowed to collect her thoughts. Then she looked up with a welcoming smile, turning serious, gray-green eyes on her students.

"Another day has been given to us," she said, raising one hand in blessing, "and we have received it gratefully and with dignity. Now is the time to report on your studies. Who would like to begin?"

They looked on her in wonder, as they always did. The lengthening shadows made her cheeks look pale and soft as silk, while the lamps cast coppery highlights on the cropped waves of black hair. The short hair and white sari proclaimed her status as a widow. But she was no ordinary widow. She was a *pandita*, a scholar and holy teacher. And she was *their* pandita. The beloved one who had rescued them, who had saved their lives and made them feel like real people again. Shyly, the girls began to speak in turn.

Pandita Ramabai was watching them, too, as they cleared their throats and reported on their classwork and their chores. She was a good listener, and she responded to each of them as they talked. As the discussion moved around the circle, she couldn't help thinking of each girl's story.

All the girls had two things in common. They were all Brahmin Hindus, members of the highest caste of Indian society and followers of the Hindu religion. And they were all widows, child-widows. Each of them had been married off to an older boy or man, perhaps even a very old man, when they were just a baby or a toddler. And that husband had died, leaving each girl—even the ones who had not yet gone to live with their husbands—a widow.

The laws of society said that widows must shave their heads, give up colored clothes and all jewelry, and never remarry. Some of the widows' families believed they were to blame for their husbands' deaths—maybe they had done something bad in a former life and their husbands were made to pay the price. The law said that the girls belonged to their husbands and their husbands' families, and now that the husbands were dead, they were as good as dead, too. So the child widows were often punished and made to suffer for their dead husbands. Maybe, they believed, maybe if they were very good and did not complain about their punishments, their husbands would be forgiven in heaven and the widows might be given a second chance in their next life. So they tried to endure.

But, oh, what sufferings they were asked to endure! The pandita looked around the circle, nodding and smiling to the girls as they talked, but inside her heart cried for each of them.

There was little Tara, only eleven years old. Her head was shaved like all the other girls, and the pandita could see where she had been branded with hot irons on her neck and shoulders—punishment for having a dead husband.

Lakshmi sat next to Tara, holding her hand like she might do with a little sister. Like many of the other girls, Lakshmi had been given in marriage to an old man when she was just a baby, and had been sent to live with her mother-in-law. When her husband died, her mother-in-law refused to feed her, began to beat her, and sometimes hung her from a metal ring in the ceiling for hours at a time—punishment for having a dead husband.

Then there was Gangabai, a beautiful fifteen year old. Because Brahmin girls were not allowed to learn to read or write, it was easy for Gangabai's brother-in-law to steal his dead brother's estate away from her, even though some of it should have belonged to his widow. She didn't know how to defend her rights, so when the family kicked her out of her own house, she had to beg for food on the streets—punishment for having a dead husband.

The pandita remembered her first conversation with Gangabai, who had knocked at the door of the school one day. The girl was starving and could barely speak. Now, after six months at the school, she was a leader there, a good student and a hard worker. All the younger girls looked up to her.

"It is for them that I founded this Sharada Sadan, this House of Wisdom," the pandita thought as she listened. "These girls have so much to offer—to God and to each other!" She prayed a silent blessing on the precious girls in her circle and smiled at them again.

"Good," she said when they had finished their reports. "You are all doing well in your classes. Tara, your reading skills are excellent, and Lakshmi, I am pleased with how quickly you are memorizing those poems. And I am most pleased with all of you because of your characters. Today I saw several acts of kindness beyond your required service." She paused. "We who have suffered greatly must seek to alleviate the suffering of others."

They looked down, but nodded silently. Then Tara leaned forward. "Pandita, please, before bed, might we have a story?"

"Yes!" Manoramabai chimed in. "Our reports were short tonight, Mother. Do we not have time for a story, perhaps about Grandfather Pandit?"

Ramabai smiled at the nickname. Her daughter had learned the title "Grandfather" when she went with her mother to England a few years ago. And Mano's grandfather was a *pandit*, a teacher, just like his daughter was a pandita. It was right to speak of him to these girls, for he was the one who had inspired her work. He was a good man, and a good example to follow.

She took a breath as she thought of him and began to speak quietly. "Like Mano said, my father was a pandit, and he had many followers who came to study the Sanskrit language and the Hindu Scriptures with him. Following custom, his family arranged for him to marry my mother when she was nine years old."

The girls nodded. It was a common story.

"But when he discovered that his young wife could not read our holy writings even though she was very smart, he was distressed," the teacher continued. "It was shameful to deny a person spiritual knowledge just because she was female! So he decided to teach her himself."

This was an unexpected twist. The girls looked up sharply and leaned in closer to their teacher.

"My mother was a good student and learned very quickly. But my father's family considered his actions a disgrace. They insisted he abide by the customs of our caste." She shook her head sadly. "Father strongly believed in justice and simply could not give in to their wrong ideas."

"What happened?" the girls wanted to know.

Ramabai spread her hands. "People began to talk. He lost all of his students. And his parents refused to support him. So he and my mother left his hometown and built a house in the forest that they filled with wonderful books. His reputation spread, and soon he had students living and studying with him again. And that is where I was born, with my sister and brother. My father and mother were determined that their girls would not grow up like she did. And so they taught all three of us everything they knew. They refused marriage offers for my sister and I, wishing for us to be scholars instead."

"But you did marry," Gangabai prompted.

"Not until I was 22," Ramabai explained. "For years, the five of us worked together, traveling the country and reciting the Hindu teachings. You are all too young to remember, but there came a very great famine and many people lost everything. My parents refused to shame their caste by begging. Eventually, they all died, my parents and sister first, and then my brother later."

"I am sorry, Pandita," whispered Tara. Her large eyes shone with tears.

Ramabai reached across to touch her hand. "Thank you."

"And that is when you married?" asked Gangabai.

"It was shortly after my brother's death. I was carrying on our work, though I was shunned by many people who felt I was responsible for my family's death. I met a kind man, a lawyer, who shared my beliefs, and we were married. But it caused another scandal."

"Why?"

"Because he was not of my caste."

The girls looked at her in surprise again.

"I was already an outcast, so what did it matter if anyone approved of our marriage?" their teacher explained. "And Bepin was a good man who supported my work. But before we had been married two years, he became ill and died. However, this time I was not alone."

She smiled fondly at Mano. "Our daughter had been born a few months earlier. We had named her Manoramabai, because she was our 'hearts' joy.'"

Impulsively, the girl got up and came to sit on her lap. Ramabai wrapped her arms around her. Her daughter was beautiful, smart, and big-hearted. She had a mother who dearly loved her. She had traveled to England and America and had never known the grief these other girls had known. The teacher knew these girls who shaved their heads to mark them as widows often glanced with envy at Manoramabai's long, shining hair and the silver combs holding it back. But they loved her like a sister. And she returned their love. Together, this group of outcasts had become a family.

But Ramabai felt she had spoken too long about her own past. "Anyway," she said, speaking briskly again. "I learned to see the world differently because of Mano's 'Grandfather Pandit.' And that is my hope for all of you. It is why we are serious about our studies and about our service to one another. It is a good lesson for us to consider as we retire for the night."

Lakshmi had been quiet all during the story, but now she spoke timidly. "Pandita? Do you think we might sing together first?" She was twisting the edge of her sari in her hands. "I know that wives and widows are not supposed to sing like unmarried girls. But, my heart is so full of many emotions tonight, and I think it would help to sing. Would that be a terrible sin?"

Ramabai swung Mano from her lap and rose to her feet. "I think it's a wonderful idea, Lakshmi! You pick a song. I'm sure we'll all know it."

Immediately the girls all stood and joined hands. Though the melody was simple and none of the students sang loudly, their teacher saw the pleasure of music dancing in their eyes. She could not suppress a smile as she joined her voice with theirs. "Telling stories and singing together—why, we are getting unruly in this school of ours!" she thought. "We're going to turn the tide and make such things honorable again!"

The next morning, Ramabai and Mano rose at four o'clock like they always did. They got up while it was still dark so they could spend an hour in prayer together before their work started at dawn. But before they sat down on the carpet in their sitting room, Ramabai made sure the door was open to the hallway. To get the authorities to let her open her school, she had agreed not to teach the Bible to her students or stop them from worshiping their Hindu gods. But she did not hide her devotion to Jesus. She hoped that the students would see her praying with Mano and be curious about her God, so she always left the door open. Sometimes one or two of the girls would join them.

This morning, it was Gangabai who crept in just as they were settling down on the carpet. Manoramabai and her mother took turns reading from a leather-bound Bible. Then they took turns praying aloud, sometimes reading prayers from a second book and sometimes saying their own words.

Gangabai listened quietly with her eyes closed, not wanting to intrude on their worship. Their voices were soft and sweet, asking their God to provide for them and to bless each of the students. When they mentioned Gangabai by name, she felt Mano's little hand reach out to take hers. She suddenly felt like she belonged in that small warm circle sending prayers up from the carpet into the holy place beyond the dark morning sky.

By the time they had finished, a question had formed on Gangabai's tongue. "Pandita," she said as they got up to begin their work, "you are a holy woman raised by a holy man who taught you the Hindu scriptures. Why did you give up our gods for the Christian one?"

The pandita gave Gangabai her full attention. "What an intelligent question. Well, it did not happen overnight. The first time I questioned our religion was during the great famine, when my father took our only food to the temples of the gods. If they were real gods who cared for their followers, they would have blessed my father for his gifts and provided food for us, too. But they didn't."

Gangabai was listening intently. Mano put the prayer books on a table and came to stand beside her friend.

"Later, my husband and I learned of the Christian religion and studied it a little," the teacher continued. "But we thought we would have to stop being Indian to become Christian. After he died, my grief was deep. I read the Bible carefully. Then I met a Christian missionary who said I did not have to give up my culture because the Christian God is the creator of every culture and he wants me to serve him where he has placed me. And I discovered the great blessing of being a woman."

"Blessing?" cried Gangabai, stepping back in disbelief.

"Yes, blessing," Ramabai repeated firmly. "The Hindu Code of Manu makes us think it is a curse to be a woman, doesn't it? It teaches that a woman must never do anything on her own, even in her own house. That she is always at the mercy of men. That her husband can replace her if she doesn't give him sons. That a man enters heaven by observing the rites of the gods, but the only way a woman enters heaven is by worshiping her husband as a god—even if he is destitute of all virtues! That she is unworthy to read or even pronounce a word of Scripture. And that widowhood is a punishment for crimes committed in a previous life."

Gangabai burst into tears. "This I know too well! After my brother-in-law stole my husband's house and left me with nothing, I had no hope!" Her voice dropped to a whisper. "I wanted to kill myself, Pandita. My life was no longer worth living. But I couldn't do it, because I was afraid. I was afraid that the punishment for the crime of killing myself would be to come back in a future life as a woman again! And I would just start over with new miseries."

"Oh, Gangabai, I understand why you felt that way," said the pandita, drawing the girl into her arms. "Many of us have had those same thoughts. But that is why I tell you that being a woman is a blessing, because it led me to a great discovery! When I studied the Christian scriptures, I discovered that Jesus honors all women, little girls, married and unmarried women of all ages. Unlike the Hindu gods, he does not value us based on our relations with fathers or husbands. Instead, he invites us to be heirs of his kingdom just like men."

Gangabai pulled away to look at her. "Just like men?"

"Yes, as equals. He calls us 'daughters of God.'"

"Daughters of God," Gangabai breathed. She looked at Manoramabai, who nodded her encouragement.

"The Christian Scriptures are open for all to read, not just men," Ramabai said. "In fact, God wants women to know his Word. He did not create us to look pretty for men and give them sons as a ticket into heaven. No, he created us to worship him and to serve him with whatever gifts he has given us. And a big way to do that is to spread his message to other widows, other girls, and to the men who have not heard, too!"

"But how?"

"Like this school!" exclaimed Manoramabai. She was blotting her friend's tears with the edge of her sari.

"That's right," said the pandita. "Let me tell you about some of my friends. While I was teaching in England, I met a group of women called the Sisters of the Cross, who rescue women living on the streets. When I asked one of the Sisters why Christians care about these women, she opened a Bible and read me the story of Jesus meeting an outcast woman from a place called Samaria. The Sister talked of the 'infinite love of Christ for sinners.' I realized that Jesus really was the Divine Savior, and that no one but Jesus could uplift the oppressed women of India and every land."

"And then I went to America to visit a cousin. I saw that Christians were working to rescue and train women there, too. I began to speak to Christian groups in different cities about the needs in India, and they wanted to help. They started a foundation to raise money so Mano and I could build this Sharada Sadan."

"So you see, Gangabai," her teacher said, resting a warm hand on her shoulder, "women and men as far away as England and America are giving money and praying just for you! And they do it because they love the Christian God, who calls them to use their gifts to serve others."

Gangabai thought about this. "You have so much love and compassion, even though you have experienced so much pain. I want to know more about your god, Pandita. May I join your prayer time again tomorrow?"

She was rewarded with big smiles. "Of course!" Ramabai declared, and Mano clapped with delight.

"Thank you," she murmured. And she reached to take Mano's hand as they went out toward the open courtyard where students on kitchen duty were setting out breakfast.

Over the coming weeks, Gangabai asked lots of questions about Jesus, and joined the teacher and her daughter for prayer every day. Sometimes one or two of the other girls would join them, too, and then they would discuss what they were learning during the afternoon quiet times.

But then the complaints began. One day, Manoramabai and Gangabai were carrying water for washing laundry back from the river when they saw a large man standing in the entrance of the school. The pandita stood only as tall as his chest, but her small shoulders were squared.

"Do the other families know you are trying to subvert our traditions, trying to destroy our cultural values?" the man thundered. "You told us this was a non-sectarian school! If you don't stop forcing Christianity on students, we will shut you down."

"My students are free to follow any religion," Ramabai replied in her firm, clear voice. "The girls are allowed to wear images of their gods around their necks if they choose to. You will find the Hindu scriptures in our library."

"Next to the Bible!"

"I remind you that this is a school. The girls are here to learn, and to do that they must have access to ideas. I do not require any religious training, so no one is forced to study anything they don't believe in. But I encourage them to think about spiritual things. If they want to read the Bible, that is their decision."

"You teach them Christian prayers!"

"My daughter and I are Christians. It is our right to worship as we choose in our own home. If students want to join us, who am I to stop them?"

"Don't play games, widow," he growled. "Keep your false god and liberal ideas behind closed doors, or we'll find another school for these girls." He spun round and stomped down the steps.

Mano and Gangabai hurried toward the door, sloshing water from their pots. "What other school?" asked Mano, ducking inside.

"There isn't one," her mother said, shutting the door with a bang. "If the girls are removed, they'll just be sent back to their in-laws' houses where they will suffer. Or worse, they'll end up on the streets."

"What will you do?" cried Gangabai.

The pandita took a deep breath and turned to them with a sad smile. "Nothing," she said, reaching for Gangabai's bucket. "There is nothing to do. People will believe what they will believe, and we can't change them. We can only remain faithful."

By the end of the next week, several of the girls had been removed from the school. The local leaders on the school's advisory board feared a scandal and resigned. The newspaper published a story saying the school would soon close. And then threatening letters began to arrive, anonymous letters warning the heretic widow to stop corrupting honorable Indian society.

The pandita was strong in public and carried on with her work, but in her bed every night, she wept and prayed for her lost girls.

Mano consoled her. So did Gangabai, whose family cared so little about her that they forgot she was even at the school.

And then one afternoon, Manoramabai answered the back door and found two young widows waiting in the alley. She quickly ushered them into her mother's office, where Ramabai was seated near the window with an open book.

"You are the pandita?" one of the young women began, bowing her bare head in respect.

Ramabai rose quickly and came forward to greet them. "I am. What can I do for you, sister?"

"We want to join your community," the girl said, taking her friend's arm.

"You do? Perhaps I should tell you more about us first. We seem to be even more outcast than usual."

"Oh, but that's why we're here!" cried the second girl. "I heard some women at the temple talking about 'that dreadful Pandita Ramabai' who is friendly to widows, and, well, if there is a place where widows are welcomed, we want to be part of it!"

Ramabai's eyes widened, and then she burst into such melodious laughter that they all began to giggle. "Praise God," she said, reaching out her arms toward the girls. "In that case, welcome to our family!"

It was the first of many such requests. Other widows soon arrived for the same reasons, and eventually the Sharada Sadan had more students than before.

By the school's tenth anniversary, Ramabai decided to return to the United States and give a report to her supporters there. Because the school was growing, she would need more money. And since, thanks to the uproar, it was now known as a school with Christian sympathies, she wanted her supporters to change the original charter so that she could start offering official Bible classes.

As usual, Manoramabai was right by her side. Together they boarded a steamer to Boston. And everywhere they got up to speak, hundreds of people came to hear about their work.

"Over the last ten years, the Sharada Sadan has had 350 students," Ramabai told the crowds. "Forty-eight have become Christians. Fourteen are now teachers, and two have started their own schools. Eight have been trained as nurses, two as housekeepers, and ten have remarried to good men."

These numbers always brought applause from the crowd. And the pandita always held up a hand to stop them.

"This means everything to those girls, yes," she would continue. "But it barely scratches the surface of the need. You see, there are 23 million widows in my country." Here she would lean forward and pause for effect. "Twenty-three million. Over fifty-thousand of those are between the ages of five and nine."

These numbers stunned the crowds into silence.

"So now you understand what a great work is still to be done in India! We need you in the West to join with us to rescue these precious women and girls. I know many of you are interested in Indian culture—you appreciate our beautiful languages and collect our jewelry. And some of you are drawn to the Hindu religion— because it is strange to you and poetic. But listen to me carefully. Do not be charmed by the outside beauty of Hindu philosophy. Come to India's sacred places and see the priests who neglect and oppress the widows. See how they collect offerings from widows for the temple, and then kick them out to beg for food and shelter. These so-called sacred places have become the graveyard of countless widows and orphans!"

"No," she would continue, shaking her head. "The Bible says that pure religion is to care for widows and orphans. If anyone has done anything at all for these outcasts of society, it is those working in the name of Christ! And so I ask you, in his name, to pray for these women and reach out to them. Come to India and join our work, or support it from afar. But do not turn your backs on my sisters."

Manoramabai was now 18 years old, slim, taller than her mother, but with the same intelligent gray-green eyes and the same passions. And every speech her mother gave thrilled her as much as the first one she had heard ten years ago, back in Bombay at the National Social Congress. She thought her mother was a hero! And it seemed the people in every American city they visited agreed with her. By the time they set out to return to India, they had raised all the money they would need to expand the Sharada Sadan.

But they had no idea just how much it would expand. Shortly after their return to Pune, famine struck. Many more widows arrived seeking refuge, and Ramabai and Mano believed they should minister to all who came to them. And when an outbreak of cholera began to spread across the city, they made a bold decision. They bought a large plot of land in the country and moved the school there. Everyone helped raise the buildings and plant crops. The students took shifts cooking, doing the laundry and housekeeping, and going to school. They called the place Mukti, which means "Salvation."

With her mother's blessing, Manoramabai went to university in Bombay and to seminary in the United States. But how they rejoiced when she returned! Ramabai had missed her daughter, and she needed her help more than ever. By now, Mukti was home to 2,000 widows and orphans.

Mano soon took charge of all the teachers at Mukti. They started a trade school in addition to the Sharada Sadan and began teaching cooking, weaving, printing, carpet-making, and vegetable farming. They built a flour mill, an oil press, five printing presses, several wells, a fruit orchard, and a farm. They set up a special school for people who were blind or deaf, and a separate school for orphan boys. They turned no one away. At Mukti, outcasts were nurtured and trained to serve their neighbors as teachers, nurses, farmers, and tradespeople.

Mukti grew so large that the local government declared it an official village. And Pandita Ramabai was appointed *lambadar*, or mayor. She visited every home, and in each one she was presented with flowers and perfume and other gifts by the people she served.

Late one morning, while the students were changing shifts to go either to class or to work, Mano returned to the one-room office she shared with her mother. The day was warm. Leaning against the cool stones that framed the long window, open to Mukti's main square, she pushed damp hair off her forehead. Her thoughts were on her morning visit to one of the tiny grammar schools in the next village.

One of her tasks was to bring all the classrooms up to government standards. She regularly traveled on foot to the village schools to instruct the local teachers on how to use the lesson book her mother had written. The primer was a collection of stories and poems meant to teach children how to read. Her mother had even included some silly songs about cats that she had written when Mano was a baby. The cat songs seemed to be everyone's favorite pages of the book. Just that morning she had been singing one of them with the village children when she heard two men laughing as they passed by.

"How can a mind as great as the pandita's produce such wonderfully silly songs for kids?" she overhead the first man say. And she was impressed by the wisdom of his friend's reply: "When a door is very large, small things can go through as easily as big ones."

"That's Mother," Manoramabai thought. "Master of seven languages, but gets a whole village giggling about kittens!"

Mano had gone to her desk and was reviewing her afternoon schedule when her mother came into the office. Humming, Ramabai stripped off the soggy shawl that covered her sari and wiped her hands on it before hanging it from a hook to dry. She was looking older these days, a few wrinkles and gray hairs starting to show, but she seemed to have more energy than ever.

"I see you've been bathing the babies again," said Mano, looking up. "You don't have to do that every week, Mother. Gangabai can handle the babies without you."

Ramabai was so petite, she barely needed to stoop to kiss her seated daughter's cheek. "Of course she can. But you know I love to do it!" She dropped onto the stool across the work table from Mano and grinned. "Reminds me of when you were a baby. You splashed around so much there was more water on me than in the basin when we were done!"

Manoramabai smiled and shook her head. "Mother, you tell me that story every week."

Ramabai laughed. "So I do." She handed a telegram across the desk. "Anyway, Miss Hastie has completed her travel arrangements. Her steamer will arrive from England in three weeks and she is anxious to get to work immediately."

Mano fingered the yellow slip and furrowed her brow. "A few of the teachers are worried about her participation, since she is not a widow and has never married. They fear she cannot relate to their concerns. Of course, I'm not a widow either, but they see me differently because of the way I was raised."

"Their fears are unfounded, Mano. If millions of Hindu widows accept being single just because custom forbids them to remarry, surely it is no strange thing for Christian women to give up marriage to bring the kingdom of God to the needy!"

"I agree with you," said Mano, nodding vigorously. "And from what I remember about the last time we saw her in England, everyone will love her right away. I'll put the concern out of my head." She handed back the telegram. "Have you decided what tasks you will charge her with?"

The pandita tapped her lips thoughtfully. "Yes. But perhaps you and I should discuss it."

Mano inserted her pen into the holder on her desk and leaned her delicate arms on the wood. "What is on your mind, Mother?"

"I've been thinking about starting a rather large project," Ramabai said, turning to face her daughter squarely. "You know how your Grandfather Pandit opened the Hindu scriptures to me by teaching me the sacred Sanskrit language, though it was forbidden."

"Yes. He believed every follower of a religion should be able to read that religion's holy book."

"Exactly," her mother continued. "The first time I tried to read the Bible in our Marathi dialect—when I was first considering Christianity—it was difficult, because it is a poor translation. I want our girls to read Scripture for themselves. I want all the people of our village and all of India to read a sensible Marathi version."

She paused. "So I think it is time to go back to the original languages of the Bible and start writing a new translation. And that is where I think Miss Hastie will be most helpful. I want her to take over some of my planning and organizing duties here, working with you, so I can devote most of my time to translation work."

"A new translation of the whole Bible," said Manoramabai, leaning back to consider her mother's words. "How long would such a project take?"

"I don't know. Quite some time. But we have the printing presses right here, so as I finish each section we can begin printing the pages. Just think, Mano," she said, jumping up from her stool and pacing the small room with excitement. "Women from Mukti traveling from village to village across India, passing out Marathi Bibles and telling how Christ has changed their status from outcast Hindu widow to beloved daughter of God!"

Mano reached out to take both her mother's arms. Her face was full of emotion as she met those strong, clear eyes that had faced down crowds on three continents. "This could be the key to India's transformation," the young woman said softly.

Ramabai smiled and drew her daughter's hands to her mouth. "You have long embodied the virtue of servanthood. You already work so hard," she said, gently touching the callouses on Mano's hand with her thumb. "But I can only do this if you are willing to relieve some of my other responsibilities here at Mukti."

Mano broke into laughter and kissed the top of her mother's head. "Is there anything better I could be doing? I don't think so!" She pushed a stack of papers into a drawer and tucked her stool under the desk. "Although," she said, eyes twinkling, "I do have a shift in the kitchen this afternoon, and if I don't get over there soon, the curry will be runny again."

"Then by all means, go!" Ramabai agreed. "Gangabai asked me to check in on the sick ward before lunch anyway. We'll talk more later."

They separated outside the door, the kitchen and hospital buildings being at opposite ends of the square. But Mano suddenly turned back and squeezed her mother's arm.

"Somehow you have turned the miseries of our sisters into sweetnesses," she said gently. "It's no wonder they all adore their pandita! And so do I." And she rushed off toward the kitchen before her embarrassed mother could reply.

Pandita Ramabai spent 12 years translating the Bible into Marathi and trained dozens of "Bible women" who preached the Christian gospel across India, handing out Bibles printed on the presses of Mukti. In 1919, the British government awarded Ramabai the highest medal of honor for distinguished service to Indian education. By this time, Ramabai was in ill health, so Manoramabai traveled to Bombay to receive the medal on her mother's behalf, and also traveled to Australia and New Zealand to raise money for their work.

Ramabai intended her daughter to be her successor, but in 1921, Mano died unexpectedly. The pandita, exhausted by her labors and now without her beloved daughter's support, quietly appointed Miss Lissa Hastie as head of Mukti. Ramabai died April 4, 1922, and was buried in the village cemetery outside of Mukti in a grave marked with a simple wooden cross. The following day, American supporters received a telegram that read, "Ramabai promoted."

Mukti continues to serve the needy people of India. But Ramabai has been largely forgotten as her country's most powerful social reformer.

Princess Ka'iulani: Hawai'i's Hope

MARCH 1, 1893. NEW YORK CITY.

A GLOOMY SKY hung low over the harbor, where the chilly wind whipped the gray water into choppy waves. But the crowd gathered on the pier alongside the newly-arrived oceanliner *Teutonic* hummed with a warm current of excitement.

Most of the onlookers were reporters, sent by their newspapers to cover the second biggest story of the week. The biggest story was the inauguration, four days from now, of Grover Cleveland as President of the United States. But second only to that news was the anticipated arrival of a princess, the heir to the throne of a small island kingdom in the North Pacific currently embroiled in a dispute with the U.S. The reporters had their notebooks open, ready to jot down their first impressions.

One reporter chewing on a long cigar leaned across the large camera set up next to him on a wooden stand. "They say she's a primitive chiefess," he said to the photographer. "Get your flash ready. You don't want to miss her bone necklace and animal skins!"

The photographer laughed.

Slowly, the *Teutonic's* gangplank lowered, creaking. A small group of Europeans exited first, clearing the way for a slender young woman, who stepped forward to address the crowd. The reporters stumbled back in confusion, the cigar tumbling into an oily puddle on the dock.

The "primitive" princess was dressed in the latest Paris fashion, her black hair swept up in an elegant twist. Her eyes were exotically large and dark, and her skin a soft caramel color, but her features were as fine and delicate as any European queen. And when she opened her mouth to speak, no one came forward to translate her native tongue.

"*Aloha*," began the princess. "Where I come from, this word means 'love,' and it is a blessing my people extend to one another both when they meet and when they part."

The reporters glanced at each other in surprise. Not only did she speak English—she spoke it expertly and with a British accent!

"Unbidden, I stand upon your shores today," she continued, "where I had thought soon to receive a royal welcome. But representatives from my land have come here asking this great nation to take away my little vineyard. They speak no word to me, and leave me to find out from rumors that they would leave me without a home or a name or a nation!"

She faced the crowd with shoulders squared, her gentle voice gaining confidence as she spoke. "Seventy years ago, America sent over Christian men and women to give religion and civilization to Hawai'i. Today, three of the sons of those missionaries are at your Capitol, asking you to undo their father's work. Who sent them? Who gave them the authority to break the constitution which they swore they would uphold?"

The reporters scribbled furiously in their notebooks, the shocked photographer jumping to get his camera at the right angle for a good shot.

"I am a poor, weak girl, with not one of my people near me and all these statesmen against me. But I have the strength to stand up for the rights of my people. Even now, I can hear their wail in my heart, and it gives me strength."

She paused, and when she began again, her words rang like bells across the water. "I am strong in my faith in God, strong in the knowledge that I am right, strong in the strength of the seventy million people in this free land who will hear my cry and will refuse to let their flag cover this dishonor to mine!"

And now the reporters could not stop themselves from openly gaping at her. She was not at all primitive or ignorant, and she had just declared that she wasn't pagan, either, but a Christian!

Her rich voice hung for a moment in the heavy air and then fell away. Fluidly, she moved aside, and the tall man behind her came forward. He introduced himself as Mr. Theo Davies, the princess's guardian in England, where she had been at school for the last several years. He announced that he would be taking questions on her behalf, and the reporters immediately began shouting questions, which he answered one at a time.

Princess Ka'iulani stood at his side, her face calm. But under her stylish wool jacket, her heart thudded in her chest. In her seventeen years, she had never before spoken in public, and certainly not about a subject so desperately important to her people. A few months ago, she would have laughed at the idea that a crowd of New Yorkers on a pier would be the audience of her first address. She had always known that she would have a prominent role in kingdom affairs and probably give her share of speeches, but the people hanging on her words would be Hawaiians and the place would be a balcony of 'Iolani Palace in Honolulu.

"What do the Americans think of me now?" she wondered. "Have I won their respect? Will tomorrow's papers champion my cause?"

She thought of the three little yellow slips tucked away in her luggage. Mr. Davies had received the three telegrams in England as they were preparing for her final tour of Europe and her jubilant return to Hawai'i. Each telegram contained one short sentence. Just eight words in all, but eight words that changed her life instantly and irreversibly.

Queen deposed. Monarchy abrogated. Break news to princess.

No more monarchy! She had read the telegrams dozens of times now, yet still the very idea made her heart race. As Mr. Davies answered questions, her thoughts drifted away from the foggy pier and back to the lush islands she had been born to rule.

She was a high *ali'i*, a member of the ruling class of chiefs. Her father, Archie Cleghorn, was a Scottish businessman who had settled in Hawai'i some years ago. But her mother, Princess Likelike, was one of the Four Sacred Ones, along with Uncle Kalākaua, Uncle Leleiohoku, and Aunt Lili'uokalani.

Uncle Kalākaua was the king, reigning monarch of the glistening emerald string of volcanic mountains known as the Hawaiian Islands. But he had no children. Uncle Leleiohoku had never married and died young. Aunt Lili'uokalani had been designated the king's heir, but she, too, had no children. So when Princess Likelike gave birth to Ka'iulani, the Sacred Ones rejoiced. Finally, a new generation had arrived to carry on their family and their nation's traditions!

Royalty had its perks, but it had its pressures, too, and the princess learned that at an early age. She had everything she wanted—pet peacocks, a pony named Fairy, a long stretch of beach for surfing, and the shade of a huge banyan tree on her estate where she loved to read. But like her mother and her aunt and uncles, she was raised to understand her role as royalty. She had a governess who taught her languages and geography so that someday she might rule with knowledge. She learned by watching her family that personal sacrifices were sometimes necessary for the well-being of her nation. And she saw how much the Hawaiian people loved her and looked to her to ensure their future. Even as a child, she took these things seriously.

On Sunday mornings she went to church with her family and spent the afternoons memorizing the catechism. She realized that her people depended on the monarch for spiritual guidance as well as political guidance. Someday when she became queen, she would be responsible to govern them with the Christian principles of truth and justice, living not for herself but for the sake of the thousands of islanders who trusted her.

So her life was serious, but also happy—until the year she turned eleven.

Her mother had become gravely ill. The doctors tried everything, but nothing worked. And one night, Likelike called her daughter, alone, into her dark sickroom. The sight of her mother lying still, eyes shut against the pain, was almost more than she could bear.

"I am sorry," she whispered from her pillow. "I know this is hard for you, and I wish I could make it easy. But I must tell you the truth, and I know you are strong."

"Mama, you are frightening me!"

"Shh, don't cry. You are a smart girl, and you know God is calling me to heaven. I may go even tonight. But first I have something important to tell you."

The princess stifled her sobs. "What is it, Mama?"

"I have raised you as I was raised, to serve our people as their *ali'i*. But the world is changing, dear little Ka'iulani." She released a sad sigh. "I know that you will have many happinesses. But I fear you will live far from home for a long time, never marry, and never be queen."

Ka'iulani gasped. Why would her mother say that? She must be wrong! Maybe it was just the pain talking.

But as Likelike expected, she died that night. And in her sorrow, the girl fervently hoped that everything else her mother had told her would prove to be wrong.

Two years later, her father and Uncle Kalākaua decided it was time for her to begin her formal education in Europe. If she was to be a wise ruler who understood the ways of other countries, she would have to go to school with children of other royal families. She was thrilled about seeing the big cities and ballrooms of the world, but she was tearful about leaving her beloved islands. The king said she'd be gone for only a year, but she had not forgotten her mother's dying words. What if this trip was the "far from home for a long time" that Mama had warned her about?

Now standing on the pier in New York, she knew she'd been right to fret. That day four years ago, when she'd left the pounding Hawaiian surf in the wake of her oceanliner and headed east, had been the last time she had seen her native land. Her year of education had turned into exile because of political struggles back home.

It all started with Uncle Kalākaua. To the native people, he was their beloved king. He was the "merry monarch" who threw huge *lūau* to celebrate special days. He was the first king of a sovereign nation to sail around the world. He was the first to install all electric lights in his palace. But the native people were not the only ones who lived in the islands. Over the decades since Christian missionaries had arrived, many American businessmen had settled there and opened trade centers for passing ships or built ranches to grow sugar cane in the rich volcanic soil. To them, the king was unpredictable and risky. Sometimes the decisions he made put holes in their wallets.

So the businessmen formed an organization to protest the monarchy. They called it the Hawaiian League, and their leader was Mr. Lorrin Thurston, the grandson of the first Protestant missionary to Hawai'i. They prodded and goaded and agitated until they had enough power to force the king to sign a new constitution.

The new arrangement gave the U.S. first rights to buy Hawaiian sugar, and also reserved the harbor at the mouth of the Pearl River for the use of American naval ships. But the thing that upset native Hawaiians the most was that though Kalākaua was still king, important government decisions now would be made by elected officials—and the only people who would be allowed to vote in those elections were landowners. Most of the natives didn't own land. A paper deed to a piece of property meant nothing to them—they just worked the land in gratitude to God and to their *ali'i*. But the deeds meant everything to the businessmen, who had busily bought them up. Now hundreds of foreigners who were not citizens of Hawai'i but who owned land there were the only ones allowed to vote—and foreigners tended to vote foreigners into office. The government soon consisted of mostly non-citizens whose interests centered around their pocketbooks.

And while Ka'iulani was in Europe studying French and German, Uncle Kalākaua died. According to his wishes, Aunt Lili'uokalani, the last of the Four Sacred Ones, was crowned queen. Her first official act was to declare Ka'iulani her successor. The teenager, grieving another family death thousands of miles from home, was now the crown princess of the Hawaiian Islands.

How she longed to return home and start taking part in state functions! But her father in Hawai'i and her guardian in England thought she should finish her education. And Queen Lili'uokalani worried that it might be dangerous for the girl to return. The Hawaiian League was still not satisfied with their new constitution and was threatening violence.

So the princess did what she could from Europe. Her father, who served in the queen's government, kept her informed of the political situation. She and her aunt wrote many letters to each other, encouraging each other to trust God. And when the queen's husband, Ka'iulani's Uncle John, died suddenly, and the girl received a letter from her aunt, saying, "If it is the father's will in Heaven I must submit, for the Bible teaches us that 'he does all things well,'" she again grieved with her shrinking family from across the seas.

Her time in England taught her more than just languages and music and history. She grew more serious in her faith, and was confirmed in the Anglican Church. She was also introduced to the first truly poor people she had ever known, men and women and children who lived in wretched slums and worked very long hours in smoky factories. She believed a Christian who truly lived by Christian principles would not stand by as people suffered. So she and her friends became involved in charity work, raising money to help the poor. Queen Lili'uokalani was so proud of her niece's convictions that she sent donations to the work in England.

And finally, Mr. Davies convinced the queen that Ka'iulani's education was complete and that the time was right for her to go home. A magazine ran a story about the "return home of Hawai'i's Hope, to celebrate her eighteenth birthday in the land of her race."

The princess was beside herself with joy! She spent the whole Christmas holiday preparing for her final tour of Europe—which would include being presented to England's Queen Victoria—and dreaming of riding Fairy in the frothy Hawaiian surf.

Then the three terrible telegrams arrived.

It took days for Ka'iulani and Mr. Davies to sort out what had happened back in Hawai'i. What they discovered was that the native citizens had continued to ask the queen to help them get their voting rights back. But when she proposed a new constitution, Mr. Thurston and the Hawaiian League took up arms to stop her! The U.S. ambassador, assuming that the queen would fight back and the Americans would be injured, announced that any attempt to resist the Hawaiian League would be considered an act of aggression. He called in troops from the ship docked at Pearl Harbor, and soon American Marines were marching up the streets of their hostess's capital.

But they forgot that Queen Lili'uokalani was a Christian. She believed that human life was more valuable than anything else at stake, and she hated the idea that young Hawaiian boys would die trying to protect her throne. So she gathered the pastors of local churches into her palace, where their prayers covered the sound of the Hawaiian League shouting threats in the street.

Never had she had to make such a difficult decision. But she reasoned that her country had long enjoyed a good relationship with the U.S., and if she surrendered peacefully now, the American government would eventually learn about the terrible mistake their representatives had made, and hand the power back over to her. No one would get hurt, and her position as leader of her sovereign nation would be restored in time. So she resigned as queen.

And the Americans appointed one of their own the new president of Hawai'i and then hopped the next boat to deliver a request to the U.S. Congress: to annex the islands and make them part of the United States.

Ka'iulani was heartbroken by the sudden turn of events. "Forget the European tour," she told Mr. Davies from the door of his book-lined study in England. "I must go straight home."

But he shook his head and drew her into the room. "No, my dear. It is now more dangerous than ever for you to return. And anyway, there is something more important for you to do. Look at these papers."

She took the stack of American newspapers from his outstretched hand. Every one of them contained a story about how the Hawaiian people were too uneducated to govern themselves and how it would be best for them if the U.S. just took over.

Her big, dark eyes widened. "Uneducated?" she cried. "Uncle Kalākaua traveled the world and knew all the great leaders and inventors! Aunt Lili'uokalani is a famous composer! I can read and write in four languages!"

"That is exactly what I mean," he said gently. "The fight is no longer in Hawai'i, but in Washington D.C. You can go there and show the Americans how terribly wrong they are about your people."

She sank into a chair in front of the fireplace. "I'm only seventeen. Why would they listen to me?"

He shot her an encouraging smile. "Why wouldn't they listen to you, Ka'iulani? You are an accomplished young woman, brilliant and beautiful and passionate. And you are a royal princess, the hope of all Hawaiians! Isn't this what you have been raised to do?"

"You're right," she said quietly. "It is the duty of an *ali'i* to protect her people. And it is the duty of every Christian to seek truth and justice. I never imagined that my duty would take this form, but if the people of Hawai'i have put their last hope in me, I will not let them down!" She rose and went to the door, turning back regally to look at him over her shoulder. "Make the necessary arrangements, Mr. Davies."

He had done so, and now she was standing on a cold pier in New York City, her heart in her throat, hoping her presence was strong enough to save her nation and her throne.

"No more questions," Mr. Davies was telling the reporters. He held out his arm to her, and with the rest of his family following them, they descended the gangplank and ducked into a carriage waiting to drive them to their hotel.

When Ka'iulani came down for breakfast her first morning in New York, Mr. Davies had good news. "The papers love you! Many of them published the full text of your speech."

She read the accounts quickly while the waiter poured her tea. "So far, so good," she said. "If only I could meet with Mr. Cleveland."

"It is several more days before he takes office," he said, passing her a dish of pastries. "In the meantime, I think you should enjoy being a tourist. The more the American people see you and get to know you, the more pressure you will put on Congress to reject the Annexation Treaty."

"Then let's go sightseeing, Mr. Davies!"

So they did. The next day they traveled to Boston to visit Mr. Davies' son Clive, who was a student at the Massachusetts Institute of Technology. They let a reporter sit with them on the train, and she wrote a glowing story for her paper. In Boston, the princess took her first sleigh ride, laughing as they flew across the powdered snow, bells jingling. She sat for a portrait with a famous photographer. Clive and his friends escorted her to a huge reception in her honor. The papers reported her every movement, and when she arrived at Trinity Church on Sunday, a crowd was waiting for her, having read that she planned to worship there.

A magazine even published an article about her Christian faith, quoting Mr. Davies as saying, "Princess Ka'iulani is not an idle girl. She feels that her life is to be one of service to the King of Kings. It is a solemn question for you to ask yourself how you can best help Ka'iulani in this work."

When she read that, she thought, "They can help me by restoring my country and praying for me to be a good leader for my people!"

A few days after President Cleveland's inauguration, Ka'iulani took the train to Washington D.C. More reporters were waiting for her, and she answered their questions with royal poise. Mr. Davies was interviewed, too, and the next day the papers quoted him again, this time observing that though the Hawaiian flag was currently flying over the Washington hotel where the Hawaiian League men were staying, "I am told that the American flag flies over the Honolulu government buildings. A curious state of affairs!"

But the princess longed for real news about the status of her country. And a few days after her arrival in Washington, she got some—and it was good. First, she learned that one of Grover Cleveland's first acts as president was a withdrawal from Congress of the Annexation Treaty. Then she read in the papers that not only had the president told Congress to wait on the "Hawaiian question," he had also decided to send a special investigator to the islands to get the whole story. He wasn't going to just take Mr. Thurston's word about his bloodless takeover of another country!

Ka'iulani was thrilled! And her excitement grew when an invitation arrived at her hotel, asking her to come to the White House that afternoon. The Davies family, too, was invited, and they all spent the morning getting ready to meet the new president and first lady.

"I am utterly charmed, Your Highness," said President Cleveland, taking her hand as she was ushered into the White House Blue Room.

He was a substantial man, and his build reminded her of the portraits of the chiefs from whom the Four Sacred Ones had descended. She smiled and curtsied like a proper lady. "Thank you, Mr. President, and *aloha*."

He smiled warmly and stretched out his hand. "Allow me to present my wife, First Lady Frances Cleveland."

A gentle-eyed young woman in a smart afternoon gown like Ka'iulani's stepped forward. "I've been reading about you in all the papers, Princess," she said. "What a pleasure to finally make your acquaintance!"

Ka'iulani liked her instantly.

When all the introductions were finished and everyone was finding a seat in the luxurious room, President Cleveland leaned closer to the princess. "This is a personal visit, so let's not discuss politics," he said. "But—I assure you I intend to see justice done in your nation."

"That is all I seek, Mr. President," she replied.

And they settled in for a few hours of warm conversation.

Less than a week remained of her stay in the U.S., and now that Ka'iulani had been received at the White House, she was more popular than ever. The National Geographic Society threw a ball to commemorate her visit. She was the guest of honor at a fundraising event organized by a group working to get American women the right to vote. The papers continued to cover her every move—which party she was invited to, who she danced with, and how she wore her hair.

By the time she boarded the ship to return to England, one thing was clear: Americans suddenly knew a lot more about the people who lived in the little string of islands to the west. The Annexation Treaty would no longer be an easy decision for Congress.

In her cabin on the oceanliner, streaming back toward England, Ka'iulani prayed that the interest her visit had stirred would result in a quick restoration of Aunt Lili'uokalani's throne.

And in the warm waters of the other ocean that bordered America, Hawaiians celebrated their beloved princess. The U.S. investigator, Congressman Blount, had arrived in Honolulu, and the first thing he did was take down the U.S. flag. He sent away the ambassador who had called in the Marines. He began his interviews with the businessmen who had taken over the country. The citizens of Hawai'i joyfully hung Ka'iulani's picture in the windows of their homes.

It was a difficult summer for the princess in England. She kept herself busy with study and charity work and social visits, but every moment she was anxious for a new word from her aunt. October came, and with it her eighteenth birthday. She had longed to celebrate it in Hawai'i, but instead she had to read about the big party the queen had thrown in her honor.

At the end of the year, a new ambassador, Mr. Willis, arrived in the islands. Mr. Willis reported that Mr. Blount had told the president the Hawaiian people had been terribly wronged by the "missionary boys." The monarchy was to be restored. But there was one condition: Queen Lili'uokalani had to agree to pardon the men who had overthrown her government.

But Ka'iulani's aunt refused. "If they go unpunished, what will keep them from trying this again?" she argued.

Mr. Willis saw her point, but he was under orders from President Cleveland. And when he informed the Hawaiian League that they would soon be asked to return their power to the queen, they flatly refused. Instead, the temporary government declared that they were no longer citizens of the U.S. and had no allegiance to the American president.

It seemed they had reached a stalemate.

The princess's father kept her informed about everything going on at home. She was spending a lot of time reading and writing letters, and kneeling in prayer in the privacy of her English sitting room. The days wore on.

Summer bloomed, and the temporary government held an election to decide if they should become their own new nation. Since only landowners could vote, and the majority of landowners were part of the Hawaiian League, the election naturally went in favor of a new nation. On July 4, they declared themselves the Republic of Hawai'i.

President Cleveland, remembering his promise to the princess, called on Congress to respond with "honor" and "morality." But Congress voted to recognize the new republic. Ka'iulani was terribly disappointed—and furious.

And she wasn't the only one. The Hawaiians loyal to the queen went against her wishes and took up arms against the leaders of the republic. But they were quickly defeated, and the republican leaders arrested hundreds of the queen's supporters—along with Queen Lili'uokalani herself! They imprisoned her in a small room in the government headquarters, the building that had once been her palace.

Ka'iulani was now more heartbroken than ever. To comfort her, her father left his responsibilities in the islands and moved to Europe to be with her. The rumor was that the new republic was not strong enough to last. The princess lived on the hope that it would fail, and world leaders would call for a return to the monarchy.

And while she chafed, waiting for her royal aunt to finally call her home, a new American president was elected. His name was William McKinley, and he was all in favor of expanding American holdings. When he sent the Annexation Treaty back to Congress, the princess considered it the last straw.

"My people put their hope in me, and I have failed them!" she moaned to her father.

"No, no," he soothed, stroking her shining black hair. "You have worked for them and prayed for them. They have not lost faith in you."

She shook her head and brushed at her tears with her fingertips. "I have tried to be obedient and respectful to my queen, but I can do so no longer. How can I set a Christian example and encourage my people from so great a distance? It is time for me to go home."

So as Lili'uokalani was being released from prison and traveling to Washington to fight against the Annexation Treaty, Ka'iulani was preparing to return to Hawai'i.

She had been gone eight years.

It took several months to pack, sail to New York, take a train across the country, and then board another ship in San Francisco for the final leg of her journey. On November 9, 1897, she stood on the bow, watching eagerly for the hazy green speck on the horizon that would signal her homecoming. And then, magically, the mountains rose before her, and the seas flashed with blue and yellow and red fish darting among the rosy reefs, and the air turned sweet with gardenias and jasmine and orchids.

She was home. "Life here will never be the same," she whispered to herself, "but whatever happens, I will be here to encourage my people through it."

When the ship pulled up to the pier in Honolulu, great crowds of people awaited their princess with shouts of "*Aloha!*" The royal band played songs written at her birth, and friend after friend draped her with the floral wreaths called *lei*.

When she could break free of her homecoming celebration, she went for a long ride on Fairy. And then she traveled to the family mausoleum, where her mother and Uncle Kalākaua were buried.

"How the country has changed!" she thought as she drank in the familiar and yet strangely unfamiliar landmarks. She was shocked at the poverty of her people, and she knew she had done the right thing to come home. In England she had learned how to help suffering people, and she vowed to do whatever she could to improve their conditions here.

She was also surprised at how warmly the republican leaders greeted her. But they had no choice, she realized. She had been away for so long that they could not accuse her of any of their disputes. Plus, if they showed any antagonism toward the beloved princess, they risked another uprising of the people. Their power was fragile. So Ka'iulani was able to go where she pleased, and no one stopped her from diving into her plans to restore the people's farms and dignity.

When she needed some encouragement of her own, she went to visit the queen dowager, Uncle Kalākaua's widow, Aunt Kapi'olani. The old woman was an invalid now and delighted in the sweet treats the princess brought her. On humid days they sat out on the *lānai*, the broad covered porch that wrapped around the house, and delighted in the dancing breezes that carried off the hot moisture clinging to their skin.

"It must have been so difficult to watch it all transpire," the princess said when they had caught up on all that had happened while she was away. "Yet you seem so calm."

Kapi'olani patted the young woman's strong hand with her own trembling one. "It was not at all easy," she replied. Her words were slightly slurred from the series of strokes she had suffered. "I still miss Kalākaua. And how I grieve the dishonor that has been done to our *ali'i!*"

"But?" prompted her niece.

The elderly aunt shrugged her frail shoulders. "But it is out of my control. I pray that God will give Hawai'i a good and pleasant future—but it is not my place to tell him how."

Ka'iulani saw the deep wisdom in her aunt's words. But it was a struggle to live that way as she went about her work.

And disturbing news was just around the corner. In early spring, word came that the Spanish had sunk an American battleship. Two months later, American ships sunk a whole Spanish fleet stationed in the Philippines. Suddenly, U.S. navy ships began to dot Hawaiian waters. The American military had discovered what a strategic location the islands held in the vast Pacific Ocean. Ka'iulani realized that the chances of the Annexation Treaty being defeated were even less likely now.

In June, a fresh grief arose when she learned that her beloved guardian, Mr. Davies, had died unexpectedly while in England. And not six weeks later, her worst fears were realized when a U.S. ship arrived with news that Congress had finally voted on the Annexation Treaty.

Hawai'i no longer belonged to Ka'iulani's people, but to the United States.

Defeated in Washington, Lili'uokalani returned to the islands in the dead of night. Ka'iulani and other high-ranking natives met her ship at the docks in silence. They brought no flowers and sang no songs. Leaning on her cane at the top of the dark gangplank, the former queen called out a sad "*Aloha*."

In the eerily flickering torchlight, her subjects moaned back, "*Aloha*."

And as she descended slowly toward them, the people began the ancient death wail. The sound wove through the cool night, causing goose bumps to rise on Ka'iulani's arms. She threw them around her aunt and drew her into the waiting carriage. With the funeral music rising and falling behind them, they began their slow procession home.

On the day of the official annexation ceremony, Ka'iulani dressed in a black gown and went to Aunt Lili'uokalani's house. They sat together, the heavy drapes drawn against the windows, and said good-bye to the nation that had once been theirs. Meanwhile, outside the palace where Kalākaua and Lili'uokalani had been crowned, the leaders of the republic turned over the government to the new U.S. minister. As the Hawaiian flag was lowered for the last time, the members of the royal band, who had been ordered to play their old national anthem, put down their instruments one by one and fled the palace grounds.

The ex-princess was so tired. She had been suffering terrible headaches for the last few years, and after the annexation she wanted to be left alone to grieve. But she had come home to be a good example to her people, to demonstrate Christian *aloha* as she put others' needs before her own. She prayed for the opportunity to continue serving her people. And it soon came.

The native Hawaiians were still trying to get their voting rights back. They wanted the American government to recognize the votes of all male citizens—as it had been during the monarchy—and not just landowners. But the men in charge during the transition claimed that the people were too ignorant to vote. So President McKinley sent several representatives to meet with both sides and recommend the best form of government.

Ka'iulani saw her opportunity. "If we introduce the representatives to the rich native heritage of the islands and convince them that the people will always have their land's best interests at heart, we might be able to get their voting rights restored to the old way," she told Aunt Lili'uokalani. "We could win at least some form of justice for our people."

She quickly devised a plan.

Everywhere the representatives traveled around the islands, they heard about the charm and beauty of the former crown princess. So when they received an invitation to a grand dinner she was throwing at her estate in Waikīkī, they were quick to accept.

On the evening of the party, Senator and Mrs. Collum, Senator and Mrs. Morgan, and Congressman and Mrs. Hitt arrived at the palm-lined entrance to Ka'iulani's home. Dozens of other high-ranking guests—some Americans and some native Hawaiians, including the former queen—milled about, their laughter tinkling across the lawn. Tucked away somewhere, a band was playing popular tunes. In the purple twilight, colored Chinese lanterns bobbed from tree boughs. And in the middle of all the glowing finery stood the elegant princess in a richly-embroidered satin *holokū*, her favorite style of dress. The representatives were enchanted.

She chattered happily with them, regaling them with stories of her European travels, until dinner was announced. Then she led them to their assigned places at the three long tables set up on the *lānai*, each set for forty guests. A *leī* of fragrant carnations decorated each place setting. Smiling, the guests took their seats—and looked up to discover that the Americans and the native Hawaiians were seated side-by-side, and that servants were bringing out huge dishes of traditional island food!

When Ka'iulani invited Senator Collum to say the blessing, the astonished statesman recovered himself quickly. He got back to his feet, cleared his throat, and in a voice loud enough to carry across the tables thanked God for their generous hostess and the food laid out before them. Then he sat down again, and the guests turned all eyes on the princess.

She smiled graciously at them, reached for the bowl of *poi* in front of her—and scooped her fingers into the mashed vegetable.

Startled, the American guests froze. Ka'iulani could read the question written all across their faces: This elegant woman eats with her fingers?

But seated across from the princess, Mrs. Hitt winked at her and stuck her fingers into her bowl, too. The sight of the Washington high-society hostess licking *poi* from her fingers was too much for Senator Collum. He burst out laughing and followed suit, and soon everyone was eating with their hands and chatting like old friends.

Later, the servants cleared away the dishes. The band struck up their instruments again, and the guests moved out on the lawn to dance in the light of the lanterns. Ka'iulani waltzed with all the representatives, and made sure their wives danced with the handsome Hawaiian men.

When the last guests departed, contentedly weary and wishing their hostess "*aloha*," Ka'iulani threw herself down on a chair next to Aunt Lili'uokalani.

"Well?" she asked, eyes closed.

"A rousing success!" the ex-queen declared, patting her niece on the knee.

"It has been some time since I danced like that."

"And you do it so beautifully." Her aunt reached for her hand, prompting the young woman to open her eyes and sit up again.

"You have taken seriously your people's hope in you and worked hard for them," she continued. "But now it is time for you to rest, Ka'iulani, and take hope that God will bless your efforts."

"Because 'he does all things well'?"

"I still believe that. Do you?"

The princess turned her elegant head and looked at her aunt with glistening eyes. "It was hard to believe it in England, and harder still here in our beautiful, sorrowful islands. But yes, I do, Auntie. I still believe."

Though Hawai'i lost its national sovereignty, Princess Ka'iulani's charm and wisdom successfully won back the voting rights for her people so that native Hawaiians would have a say in the decision-making of their new government. But the loss of her nation and the strain of its defense had

taken a toll on the princess. Her health compromised, she died in 1899 at the age of 23.

As her mother had predicted, she never married, never became queen, and spent nearly a third of her years in exile. But she lived her short and tragic life to the glory of God, faithfully applying her Christian beliefs to political decisions and other aspects of her life. To native Hawaiians, she remains their most beloved ali'i and the embodiment of the Hawaiian spirit of aloha.

THE BIBLE IN NEW WORDS

DURING THE PROTESTANT Reformation, Christians called for new translations of Scripture. The Bible had been translated many times before. Cyril and Methodius, for example, had translated it into the Slavonic language in the ninth century. But by the time of the Reformation, when the Bible was primarily read in Latin, Protestants saw a need for everyone to read and understand it, not just people trained in old languages. So theologians began translating it into local tongues. William Tyndale (1490-1536), for example, translated the Bible into English, and Martin Luther (1483-1546) into German.

By the time of the modern period, Bible translation had become common. As missionaries traveled the world, they took with them the resources to make editions of Scripture available in the language of the local people, often creating written languages for people that had none. And often their work benefited others they could not expect. When Niijima Jō bought his first Bible, it was a Chinese translation. Though his first language was Japanese, that Chinese Bible opened up the gospel to him. The missionary translators who prepared his Chinese Bible probably didn't realize just how far their work would go!

Missionary translators were busy in the early days of the modern period. Hudson and Maria Taylor worked on their own translations and also hired translators to work for them. Robert Thomas passed out Chinese Bibles to Koreans who had none, and the missionaries that built on his work, John Ross and Samuel Moffett, produced more accurate and accessible translations for the Korean people. In Mexico, Marianna Slocum began her work of putting Scripture into the Tzeltal language. Her efforts were plagued by the difficulties of translating concepts that made sense in Middle Eastern cultures but did not seem to have equivalent ideas in Tzeltal culture. But with the help of local converts, she was able eventually to deliver the Bible to a people with no concept of a holy book.

In English, the dominant translation since 1611 was the King James Version. But during the last century, new manuscript discoveries and better knowledge of the original languages of the Bible have led to additional English Bible translations. Some of these versions are not intended to be rigorously accurate, but to communicate to modern people in a more understandable way. With new views on how to communicate Scripture in English, plus trained and eager translation teams, modern versions like the *Revised Standard Version* (1952), *Amplified Bible* (1958), *New American Standard Bible* (1971), *New International Version* (1978), *New King James Version* (1982), *Today's New International Version* (2005), and *The English Standard Version* (2001, 2007) offer strong competition.

Today, organizations like *Wycliffe Bible Translators* seek to deliver the Scriptures "to all people in the language of their heart." Over 2,200 language communities still do not have access to the Bible—so translation is sure to continue well into the future.

MARIANNA SLOCUM: PLANT THE
GOOD SEED IN YOUR HEART

1942. CHIAPAS, MEXICO.

THE THATCHED HUT was barely large enough for three men. The young one stood, feet apart, supporting his sick brother with both arms and facing down the shaman. The old holy man, half-blind and with skin like leather, had connected his people to the spirit world for many years.

"I need *posh!*" the shaman demanded, rolling his milky eyes. "*Posh!*"

The young man helped his brother to a mat on the floor. He lifted a narrow strap from his neck and handed the shaman a tight animal skin filled with liquor. The old man put the skin to his lips and drank with great gulps. When he had drained it, he shook it violently, persuading the last few drops onto his tongue.

"Can you help my brother?" asked the young man. "Can he be healed?"

The shaman ignored his questions. "Is this all you have?" he cried, flinging the bottle aside. "I need *posh* to do my work!"

"I've given you all I have. Please, can you save my brother?"

The old man grunted in disgust. He was so drunk that he felt for the pulse at the shoulder instead of the wrist. "He's not good," he diagnosed with confidence.

"How can I save him?"

"You must give part of your life for his," hissed the shaman. He grabbed at his walking stick to steady himself as he got to his feet. "This is your burden. You will take his pain to save his life." He swung the stick violently, and the blow knocked the young man to the ground. "Your life for his!" he shouted. He began to pummel the prostrated man with his fists.

A man can take only so many beatings. The idea raced through the young man's mind as he blocked his face with his arms. But this is for your brother!

Another blow to the head, and the hut began to spin. He blinked rapidly. And now, beyond the swinging fists and flinging saliva of the drunken shaman, he saw not only the body of his brother but also the body of his wife. "How?" he groaned. "How is Maria here? She is dying too?" His vision went purple, then black.

"No!" The scream startled him from sleep and he sat up quickly on his woven mat. He ran his fingers through his hair, damp with sweat, and rubbed the darkness from his eyes.

Everything seemed to be normal. The long, one-room structure he was sitting in was his house. The narrow wooden planks tied together and daubed with mud were his walls. The small bank of unlit candles on a log was his family altar. Nothing was out of order.

He began to sigh with relief, but, skittish with sleep, jumped when a beam of moonlight shifted across a clump of mud on the wall. "The shaman's face!" he thought momentarily. Then, "No, it's nothing. My dream is fooling me."

But then a new fear arose. What time was it? He peered through a chink in the wall to determine the position of the moon. Nearly morning! His sweat grew cold again. He slumped back to the mat with a loud groan.

A small hand reached across his chest. "What is wrong, Martin?" came a soft voice.

Martin swallowed hard. "I had a vision, Maria."

The young woman sat up quickly beside him, her black braids swinging. "Tell me!" she insisted.

"I saw my dead brother again. And I think I died," he said. He didn't mention seeing her body beside his brother's in the shaman's house.

"When did you dream this? During the early night? Or just now?"

"Just now."

She put her hand to her mouth to stifle a gasp. "Morning visions always come true right away!"

"I know," he said quietly.

They didn't speak for a long time. The starlight outside faded. A pink glow seeped through the cracks in the walls and grew brighter, making floating specks of dust sparkle like powdered rubies. They watched it for a while, and then Martin said, "I go to the market."

He reached for his dark, homespun poncho and pulled it over his lean body, cinching it around his waist with a sash woven in red and blue. Rising from the sleeping mat, he went to the far corner of the hut and packed a basket full of ripe green *chayotes* and piles of string beans. He lifted the basket to his back, hooked the wide strap across his forehead, and snatched a straw hat from the wall near the door.

The dream replayed vividly in his mind as he made his way, barefoot, across the packed dirt road of his village. The basket bumped behind him, his calf muscles bulging under their burden. As he passed a sun-dried hut, a neighbor stepped out for his morning stretch. They made eye contact and gave each other a quick nod, but didn't speak.

Turning his eyes back to the path, he was just in time to sidestep a wandering goat, knocking two *chayotes* out of the basket. He bent to retrieve them, and moved on past the huts and a sloping field of papery stalks. His trek continued down the stony mountain trail flecked here and there with thistles.

Below at the Yochib bush-market, where the mountain paths crossed and the nearly-dry river trickled off into a cave, he joined the other sellers displaying their wares. Maize, beans, squash, chilis, wheat, sweet potatoes, cotton, *chayote*, coffee, lengths of fabric in every color—all were piled in baskets or spread out on woven mats. Yochib was treeless and often rainy, but this time of year the sky was bright and sun-bleached. Broad straw hats flashed white across the market with every movement of merchants and customers.

Martin showed his produce to everyone who passed. "Selling is easier with enthusiasm," he reminded himself. But all he could think about was his worrisome dream. What did it mean that his wife had appeared dead? What did the shaman have to do with it? Had he put a curse on Martin's family? The questions he pondered were more frightening than the dream.

His hat seemed to be doing little to shield him from the heat. He felt the sweat collecting on top of his head and running down his neck. As the day progressed and the sun reached its highest point, the market thinned. Everyone was looking for a cooler spot to rest. He decided to join them.

He made his way along the main market street and came to one of the few trees in the area. It was an orange tree planted in front of the square stucco house belonging to the man known as Professor Villa. The professor was an anthropologist who had spent months interacting with the Tzeltal people, observing their language and customs. The locals considered him a friend.

But it was not the anthropologist Martin saw today, but a pale woman with a bob of soft brown curls. She sat on a chair under the orange tree, her buttoned white dress rippling silvery in the shade. A small group of people sat on the ground in front of her, taking advantage of the rare shadows.

She had a pleasant smile, so Martin stopped to listen. She was speaking in broken Tzeltal about a god who wrote a message in a book, and she moved around little fabric figures on a board propped next to her. She seemed to be acting out a story.

Looking up, she caught his eye, and when she finished her presentation, she walked over to him. "Hello," she said. "Did God's words arrive in your heart?"

Martin's sharp brow creased with puzzlement. "*Me'tik*," he said, using the respectful Tzeltal word for woman, "not a word arrived in my heart." He wasn't sure what she meant by the phrase, but it had certainly not occurred.

"My name is Marianna," she said, pointing to herself.

"I am Martin."

She glanced at the basket of produce on his back. "May I buy some *chayotes*?" She reached in her pocket for currency.

That Martin understood. He smiled and sorted his produce for her.

"Thank you," she said, accepting the food in her hands. "If you will come back again, God's words may arrive in your heart."

Martin gave her another polite nod. She seemed pleasant enough, if strange. Maybe if he came by next market day, she would buy more from him. He moved on toward the market again.

That night, the white woman sat in the one-room stucco house she was leasing from Professor Villa. "The Tzeltal are fossils," the professor had told Marianna when she arrived, "remnants of the Mayan people. I've been studying their various villages for years. You're welcome to use the house while I'm away, if you'll agree to keep records of what you learn. Sometimes it is months before you realize the significance of something you jotted down before bed."

So every night, as promised, she sat at the worktable with pen in hand, recording her findings. She kept a set of notes for Professor Villa and a more personal set in her journal, in case she one day decided to write a book about her work in Mexico.

She was trying to create a written language for the Tzeltal, who had never had one. All their traditions and stories were passed on verbally, from one generation to the next. "Flannelgraphs are helpful," she told herself, "but if the people could understand the Bible in their own tongue, perhaps then the good seed of God would take root in their hearts."

She put down her pen and opened the door. The night sky was clear and dark, pierced with glimmering stars and a slivered moon. The air was cold, a sharp contrast to the heat of day, and she ran her palms up and down her arms to ward off the chill.

"Oh, Bill, if only you were here," she said aloud. Her breath rose in a white plume. "You were already welcome among the Tzeltal. The closest I can get is this house in the marketplace." She shook her head. "The loneliness is getting to me. I've got to stop talking to myself."

A stone skittered past the door, its clatter loud in the stillness of the night. She leaned out and peered into the darkness. A man jumped out at her. She stifled a scream, and then immediately recognized him. In one hand, he clutched a bottle of liquor, and in the other, a machete. A rifle was slung across his shoulder. He looked so drunk he could barely stand.

She didn't want to show fear, so she stayed still. But the fine hairs on her arms stood up with alarm. "Juan Nich," she said in her sternest voice, "what are you doing here? It is late!"

"Where is Rosalia?" he shouted. "Where is she, you thief?"

"Your wife is not here. Did she run away from you again?"

"I heard you talking to someone. Is she in your house?" He spat toward her and lurched forward to peer inside.

Marianna stepped back so he could see behind her into the house. "No. I have not seen her today."

He glared into the corners, wobbling. "She is not here."

"I told you that. If you thought she was here, then you must have been beating her again. Tell me, Juan. Why do you beat your wife?"

"Because she is my wife," he growled, as if that fact gave him the right to treat her however he pleased. He spat on the doorstep again. "And it is not your business. You are not welcome here, woman. Your god is not welcome here." He flailed his machete close enough that she felt the slices of cold air on her skin. But she refused to flinch.

He spun around and stumbled off toward the road, hurling curses at her over his shoulder.

She took a deep, calming breath and watched him stagger down the moonlit hillside. "It really is too bad I cannot use any of those words for my translating," she said to make herself laugh. "He so often provides me with new vocabulary, very little of it practical!"

She shut the door firmly, barring it this time, and sat down at the table again. A small diary lay before her, and she opened it. Inside the front cover was scrawled "Bill Bentley," and the handwriting matched all the daily entries. She read a bit from it every day to encourage herself. Tonight, she turned to the passages about Bill's early days in Chiapas.

Bill had not been immediately welcomed in Mexico either. But he had made one or two acquaintances, and one day one of them, a local man named Pancho, had been injured. He had been in a fight and got slashed in the head with a machete. The wound was so deep it had exposed part of his brain. Bill was not a doctor, but he used the little medical training he had to try to keep Pancho alive. The poor man eventually died, but Bill's genuine willingness to help one of their own made him more welcome among the Tzeltal of that village.

"What am I supposed to do, Bill?" she asked aloud again. "I can't pray for someone to get hurt so I can be accepted! How else might I be welcomed among the Tzeltal? They are not as tolerant of Protestants as they were when you were here. Our people have abused theirs so much that we can't even give them the gospel."

She held up a photo she kept in the back cover of the diary. Bill's grin beamed from the paper, his strong jaw softened by the friendly smile. She remembered his broad shoulders, how confident he was, how he loved to laugh. Her memories of him always took her back to their first days together at Camp Wycliffe in Texas.

She had just graduated from college and her interest in languages suggested that translation work might be the right next step in her life. A man named Cam Townsend had started a camp to train potential Bible translators, and she signed up. Bill was one of the young men who unloaded her luggage when she arrived. As they got to know each other, he revealed that he wanted to marry someone dedicated to mission work in Mexico. Well, dedication is what kept her there, she insisted, working hard to graduate from translation boot camp. But it didn't hurt that the handsome young missionary had taken an interest in her.

When Bill proposed to her, Marianna imagined an almost magical future. She and Bill would work side by side, laboring to deliver the gospel to people who had never heard it before. They would walk the dusty hills telling stories of Jesus and inviting the locals into their home for beans and tortillas. She imagined their children growing up there, learning the language and customs like natives, carrying on their work for generations to come.

But such dreams were not to be. Six days before their wedding, while making their final preparations at her family home in Pennsylvania, Bill had a heart attack in his sleep. The minister who was going to do their wedding did Bill's funeral instead. His body was sent back to his family's home near Topeka, Kansas. Later she wept over his grave, where the new headstone read: *William C. Bentley, 1913-1941, Ambassador for Christ to Mexico.*

She quickly decided that the work he had started in Mexico was too important to end with his death. She would finish her training and carry on with their plans, though he would no longer be at her side.

"Well, I'm here, Bill," Marianna said, slipping the photo back into the diary. "I can only believe that God will send me someone to help me connect with our people. I'll just keep praying."

She changed into her nightdress and climbed into her sleeping bag on the army cot. As she did, the generator of her Coleman lamp suddenly gave out. "Again?" she mumbled into her pillow. "I need to replace that lamp. It's going to be another dark and cold night."

When she opened her door to the early sun on the next market day, Marianna found several people waiting for her. Word was getting around that she was dispensing medicine, and she gladly helped as much as her supplies allowed. By late morning, her visitors were gone and she had eaten her usual breakfast of *chayote* and a mug of coffee. She took her flannelgraph out to the spot under the waxy green branches of the orange tree and waited for the crowd to gather in the shade.

Only a few people passed by, so she went back to the house for her small stash of secret weapons. They were small square boxes for playing records and phonographs, made by the Victor Talking Machine Company. Few Tzeltal people had ever seen a Victrola, and Marianna found that playing one outside her house captured the attention of people passing by. Several Wycliffe translators had helped put together recordings of the Bible in a Tzeltal dialect, and the locals were amazed to hear their language coming out of a box. Sometimes they would sit for hours, listening. Marianna had also used it to get them interested in learning how to read their language—that is, if she was ever successful in working out a written vocabulary.

She wound up the Victrola and put on the gospel record. Sure enough, people began to gather under the tree to fan themselves and listen. To her surprise, Martin the produce seller showed up again. He seemed mesmerized by the talking box and edged closer to it. She recognized Juan Nich at the back of the crowd, too. He looked more sober than he had the last time she had seen him, but his eyes were fixed on Martin in a way that made her uneasy.

When the record finished, she got up to speak with Martin, but he was quickly returning to his spot at the marketplace. Some of the others remained in the shade and looked at her expectantly. So she picked up her flannel figures and began to tell another Bible story in her halting Tzeltal.

She continued with her mid-day Bible stories, excited that Martin appeared every week on market day. And finally, one day, when everyone dispersed to go back to their work, Martin remained. She smoothed the wrinkles from her dress and stood up to greet him. "It's Martin, right? Hello again."

"Hello, *Me'tik*."

"I'm so glad you returned. Do you have questions about the record or the stories?"

He moved closer, and when he spoke, his voice was low. "I need your help."

"What kind of help?"

He sat cross-legged on the ground, his produce basket beside him, and Marianna joined him in the thin grass that grew only in the shade of the tree.

"My first wife died young," he began. "I think a shaman put a curse on her. I lit thirteen candles on the altar in my house. I knelt before a cross and prayed. I wanted to save her, but she died."

"I am sorry," she said gently. Her Tzeltal phrases were limited. She hoped she had used this one correctly.

"Then, not long ago, my brother became very sick. Shamans can curse us, but they can sometimes heal as well. So I took him to many shamans, hoping one could lift the curse. One offered to help, but only if I brought *posh*. So I did. Shamans cannot work without *posh*."

"So I hear."

"He checked my brother's wrists and then beat me, saying it would remove the curse."

She frowned. "Beating you would remove the curse from your brother?"

"That is what he said."

"Did your brother live?"

Martin's hard swallow gave her the answer. "He died many weeks ago."

"I am sorry," she said again. "But if your wife and your brother are dead, my medicine is of no value. How else can I help?"

"I fear that the shaman, or someone who pays a shaman with *posh*, will curse me or my new wife." Martin cupped his hands over his eyes. "I have not slept in days. I see our deaths in my dreams."

"Oh, you are living in fear!"

He nodded. She saw his strong jaw tighten as he held back his distress.

"Martin," she said gently, "perfect love casts out fear." She spoke carefully, in her best Tzeltal, but she could see Martin was puzzled. "Jesus can set us free," she tried again.

"I do not understand."

"It is all right." She considered another idea. "I also lost someone I loved, Martin. His name was Bill. A few days before we were married, his heart gave out." She hoped that what she was telling him made sense in Tzeltal. "At first, I was afraid. But I found relief from my fear. I found that relief in my God, Jesus. That is why I am here. I've come here to tell you about him."

Martin bobbed his head, acknowledging that he had understood at least some of what she'd said.

"I will pray for you, ask my God to protect you from any curses," she said.

"Thank you, Marianna *Me'tik*."

She smiled at that and wondered what Bill would have thought of her being called "Marianna Woman." She rose. "Please come back again, Martin. I hope that my stories can help the Word of God arrive in your heart. It is a good seed to plant in your heart. It will grow if you give it time."

He nodded again. "I will come back."

Martin began to stay for a few minutes every afternoon after the other visitors dispersed. Marianna read to him from the Bible, trying to translate the parables of Jesus and other stories into concepts from Tzeltal culture. But it proved a difficult task. Martin's people did not have words for certain concepts she thought were simple, like "left" or "right." So to communicate stories about people living so long ago in a land far across the ocean was a great challenge. It was even harder for Marianna because some of the Catholic missionaries that came before her had tried to tell the Tzeltal people about Jesus, but the people had been confused and mixed the message of the Bible with some of the ancient Mayan beliefs their ancestors had passed down. She and Martin had a lot to untangle.

One day, when he couldn't remember something she had taught him during their previous discussion, he said, "*Me'tik*, I am sorry. I lost the word out of my heart."

Marianna sat up a bit straighter on the scraggly grass. She always listened as closely as she could to every word he spoke, looking for useful Tzeltal vocabulary. This last phrase intrigued her. She decided to try it out herself. "Martin," she said slowly, "when we believe in the Lord Jesus, God loses all our sins out of his heart."

Martin's dark eyes widened with understanding. "God loses our sins out of his heart? This is what forgiveness means?"

"Yes!" She was exuberant. "Yes, that is forgiveness."

"More," he said, leaning forward and forgetting about his basket of produce. "Tell me more."

She explained that God forgives his children because his son Jesus sacrificed himself so they wouldn't have to.

"Yes, the gods accept sacrifice to pay for our bad things," he replied.

She explained that the God of the Bible was the one who created the sun and moon.

"Our ancestors taught us to worship the sun. Your God rules over that god?" he said with amazement.

She explained that the God of the Bible rules all of creation, and all the spirits obey him.

"Even the shaman's spirits?" he wanted to know.

"Yes, the shaman's spirits are at war with God," she answered. "But he is more powerful than they are. That is why he deserves to be worshipped."

"I understand!" He grinned at her, and his glance fell on the basket. "Oh, I must finish at the market. More next time!"

As the weeks continued, Martin's interest in the Christian gospel grew and his fear of the shaman faded. He even invited his wife to hear Marianna's message. But that evening, as he was bringing into their hut the fruit to sell the next day, he asked Maria what she thought of the story Marianna had told them with her fabric figures.

"Why do you care so much what the white woman says?" Maria replied. She was scraping the flesh out of a pile of roasted *chayotes*.

"She brings us the message of Jesus."

She shrugged. "It is not the tradition of our people."

He dropped his arm-load of produce into the big basket in the corner and turned to face her. "It is the message of life," he insisted.

"Our people are ancient, Martin. Have they been wrong for so many generations?"

"It seems so! Only God can write our names in the Book of Life in Heaven," he said, his voice rising. "Do you not want him to write your name?"

She threw down the bowl of *chayote* paste and moved toward the door. "I do not believe any of this is true."

He grabbed her arm and pulled her back, his strong fingers digging into her skin. "Maria, listen. If your name is not written in the book—."

She spat on the floor and knocked his hand away. "No more, Martin!" She turned toward the door again.

His neck and jaw tightened with anger. "Listen to me!" he shouted, and struck her across the face. As soon as he did, he froze, and stared at his outstretched arm like it was an unknown intruder.

Maria touched a hand to her lip and saw a smear of blood on her fingers. With a sob, she burst outside and ran toward the hut of a friend.

He shut his eyes and took a deep breath, trying to quell the shock of his outburst. This was not what he had meant to happen. He thought for a moment, and then jumped past the open door and ran through the village. He scurried down the hillside, sending rocks and clods of dirt bouncing off the trail. All the way to Yochib he ran, through the deserted marketplace and past the leafy orange tree, until he knocked on Professor Villa's door. He needed to tell Marianna what had happened and ask her what to do.

"Oh, Martin," she said, her eyes sad. "It is right to speak to your wife about the message of God. But a man should never strike his wife. If you ask him to, God can lose the anger from your heart. And he can lose the memory of your sin from his heart."

"Help me," he pleaded.

They sat outside the house and prayed together. When the sun began to slide behind the mountains, she sent him home to find his wife and confess his sin to her as well.

Daily, Martin learned to change old behaviors that he now knew were against the message of God. He had already learned that he could not bully another person into accepting God's salvation.

He also used to drink a lot of liquor and found himself in fights. Then Marianna told him the story from Bill's diary about Pancho's death and explained how a life of love involves self-control. Martin became more concerned that his life look like Christ's life.

Some of his friends did not like the changes Martin made to his way of life. But others wanted what he had, including Maria. When he had apologized for striking her and told her his God would not allow such behavior, she was willing to hear more about this God. She even agreed to go with him to hear Marianna's afternoon lessons.

The weather turned cool and rainy in Yochib. In the afternoons when he wasn't working in the fields, Martin made his way down the mountain to Marianna's house. They would sit at a table on the small porch and discuss the meaning of Tzeltal words. Martin wanted to help Marianna find just the right words to explain the message of God to his people.

"No," he said, shaking his head as she read him a passage she had recently translated. "That will not be understood."

"How do I say wholehearted?" she asked.

"Of one heart."

"How do I say a person is just or righteous?"

"A straight heart."

She scribbled his phrases on her stack of notecards.

"Yes, put the words where you will remember," he agreed. "It is very important that you get this right. This is the Word of God."

She laughed. "Yes, it is. I'll try to get it right."

"My people are descendents of a great nation, you know. Our teachings are a part of who we are."

"I know. And it is important that I learn more about your people's beliefs. In the past, when others told you about the Bible, some ideas became combined with your ancient stories. I do not want that confusion to happen again."

"Yes. So you must use just the right word or the whole message may be lost. For example, I have heard you say 'God in Heaven'"——

he pointed to the sky—"but my people might think you mean the sun god."

"Good to know. Thank you!" She wrote "God in heaven" on a card and drew a line through it.

Hearing a shout from the road, they looked up. It was Maria, coming toward them with a scarf tied over her head. The fine rain had stopped an hour ago but the air was still thick with moisture.

Martin stood up, frowning. "She was busy weaving with the other women when I left. Something must be wrong." He went to meet her. They quickly returned to join Marianna on the porch.

"Martin, Juan Nich is looking for you," Maria gasped, out of breath. "They say he wants to kill you!"

"It is a dispute from long ago," he explained to the missionary. "I suspect it was he who paid the shaman to curse my brother."

"Is he drunk?" asked Marianna.

Maria nodded. "Yes, *Me'tik*. What if he puts a curse on us?"

"He cannot," Martin declared. But he had begun to sweat. Marianna could see he was fighting off his old fears again.

"But your brother, and your first wife! They died of curses!" Maria was twisting the ends of the long scarf in her brown hands. "And you had a dream that something bad was going to happen. Maybe it was this!"

He remembered the dream. He had begun to forget it, in his joy of learning about the God who wrote a book for his people, but now images from his dream flashed in his memory. He swallowed hard and shut out the images, wanting his wife to see how much he trusted Jesus. "My God is stronger than the shaman's curse," he insisted. "He removes curses."

"Do you wish to stay here tonight?" Marianna offered.

"Yes, maybe that is a good idea!" Maria said, her eyes brightening.

Martin thought for a bit. "No. Juan would find us here anyway. I am going to go home."

Maria tugged his arm. "But what if he finds us there! He will kill you!"

"I will trust in my God," said Martin. "Besides, if I run and hide, he will just look for me and I will have to live in fear. Better to face him now."

"Are you sure?" asked Marianna.

Martin smiled calmly. "Yes, *Me'tik*."

"Then take this with you." Marianna ducked inside the house and came back with a Victrola. "Keep it. Play it. Think on the things of God and pray for him to protect you."

He took the box in his hands. "Thank you."

"You remember how to use it?"

"Yes."

"Good."

They all looked at each other.

"Then go in peace, my friends," Marianna said, putting a hand on each of them. "I will pray for your safety. And if I do not hear from you tomorrow, I will come up the mountain and check on you—even if your village is not ready to welcome me!"

They gave her grateful smiles and set out for the road.

Marianna knew that they had long lived in fear of curses, and fear is not easy to overcome even when a person wants to be rid of it. She prayed for them while she fixed rice for her supper. Then she worked on her translation for a few hours. But she was too distracted to make much progress, so she set her notes aside, wrapped her sleeping bag around her shoulders, and sat down on her knees to pray. Even after she went to bed, she found she couldn't sleep.

She trusted in God to protect her friends. But she also believed that God ordains the end of a person's life as he does the beginning. There was no guarantee that Juan's machete and rifle were not part of God's plan for Martin and Maria.

And a selfish thought nagged at her, too. "Martin is the one who has trusted me here, who is helping me learn to communicate with these people. What will I do if he dies?" She told herself to trust God to provide for Martin, and for her. And she waited for the sun to rise.

As soon as it was light enough, she set out to climb the hillside toward Martin's village. She wasn't sure of the way, but she just couldn't wait any longer to learn what had happened. She knew the village was partway up the mountain, and she knew where that trail began. It was steep and winding, but also well-traveled, and she figured if she followed it carefully, she would eventually find the right place.

"Thank God it isn't raining this morning," she said aloud. In fact, the sun was rising up the mountain with her, gaining on her, and she was grateful for her hat.

She was halfway up the hillside when the silhouette of a man appeared in the brightness above her. She held on to her hat with one hand and tilted her head back to get a good look.

"Martin?" she cried.

"Yes, *Me'tik*. It's me." He scrambled down the path toward her.

"You're all right! What happened?"

"I sat in the hut all night. I prayed to God. I played the box. If Juan came to kill me, I wanted to die giving the gospel."

"But he never came?"

"No." He beamed at her. "Maybe he fell asleep. Or changed his mind. Either way, God's angels protected me!"

"Praise God!"

"I no longer believe in curses, *Me'tik*. I believe in God only. And I want you to come to my village and tell everyone."

"I would love nothing more."

"Will you come now?"

"Yes!" She laughed. "If you're inviting me, of course I will!"

"I will carry the box on my back. We will play it so my village can hear our language coming out of the box. We will tell them about the God who defeats curses." He started up the trail again, his nimble feet avoiding the loose rocks, and looked over his shoulder at her. "Come!" he shouted, waving enthusiastically.

Marianna laughed again and picked her way up the hillside behind him. "I'm no longer alone, Bill," she thought. "The seed you planted is breaking through the soil! Do you see it growing?"

They reached a plateau and Marianna saw the cluster of huts on the far side of a small cornfield. As they got closer, Martin began to shout. The children appeared first, chasing each other and fighting for the best view of the visitor. Then a dozen or more curious men and women came toward them, some toothless and withered, some straight-backed and muscular. She gave them a warm smile as they gathered around her and stared.

"Marianna *Me'tik*," Martin said, pointing to her. "Listen to her!" Then he spread his arms wide. "She has come with God's Word! It is a good seed to plant in your hearts."

Juan Nich did not trouble Martin again. Martin introduced Marianna to his people, and together they traveled to the nearby villages, playing the Victrola and teaching the Bible. Though she faced more than one threat, including the burning down of chapels and the murder of one of her converts, Marianna's work among the Tzeltal people grew. And in 1947, Florence Gerdel, a nurse, joined her as a partner in ministry. Within a few years, they had made several hundred converts and completed a Tzeltal translation of the New Testament.

Christian Tzeltals eventually asked Marianna and Florence to move among them in Corralito, where they built a church. And when that work was established, they began yet another one in Colombia.

DIETRICH BONHOEFFER: COSTLY GRACE

JULY 20, 1944. EAST PRUSSIAN FOREST OF RASTENBURG (NOW KETRZYN, POLAND).

THE SUN BORE down with glaring intensity. Below the thick forest canopy, the light was soft and shadowy, and the air cooler. But sweat collected beneath the brims of the soldiers' caps. They stood at attention as their commanding officer performed his inspection. His own gray uniform was sharply pressed. He walked tall, one arm bent behind him, as rigid and angular as the black swastika emblazoned on his red armband. "You are the best of Germany. You will not disappoint the Führer!"

"*Jawohl*, Herr Commandant!" they replied as one. Yes, sir!

Satisfied, he fell into place at the end of the line of troops, facing the concrete bunker. He scanned the nearby barracks and the moss-covered trees beyond. The *Wolfsschanze*, or Wolf's Lair, was a secure stronghold, buttressed with acres of forest and a series of barriers and fences. But the commandant kept a watchful eye. If the Führer's life was at stake today, his would be, too, and he did not intend to fail.

A door swung open and a small crowd of uniformed men came down the walkway. The man in front had a face known around the world. Only one other man, the silent film comedian Charlie Chaplain, was so easily identified by that little mustache, like a blackened toothbrush on guard duty against potential sneezes. But that was the only similarity. Unlike Chaplain, Adolf Hitler was not known for his sense of humor.

The commandant could tell this was an important meeting by the number of top officers with the Führer. He recognized Field Marshal Keitel, General Heusinger, and Colonel Brandt, among others. Their steps rang across the pavement, light glinting off the medals of honor pinned over their hearts.

With a signal from the commandant, the guards clicked their heels and thrust out their right arms, fingers together and palms flat. "*Heil*, Hitler!" they shouted.

The procession entered a small outbuilding, where the commandant had secured a conference room. But another man soon came down the path toward the small bunker. He was also festooned with medals, and bore other marks of bravery, including an eye patch and the empty, dangling right cuff of his uniform. The commandant knew this man, too—Lieutenant Colonel Claus von Stauffenberg. It was well known that he had lost an eye and a hand in the Allied attack in North Africa.

The commandant rushed to open the door for the colonel, who carried a sturdy briefcase in his only hand. Field Marshal Keitel met them at the conference room.

"My apologies, sir," said Stauffenberg. "My plane just landed and the staff car was delayed. Am I very late?"

"We are just getting started. Come."

They went in together. A massive, solid oak table crowded the room. Hitler was seated in a high-backed chair at the center, his advisors filling out the remaining places. Keitel announced the arrival of the final member of the group, and motioned for the commandant to get the colonel a chair. The guard nodded toward an empty place along the wall.

But Stauffenberg leaned in to Keitel and whispered loudly. "Would it be possible for me to sit closer to the Führer?" He gestured toward his ear with his empty jacket cuff. "My hearing is another thing I left in North Africa."

Keitel gave a wordless order and the commandant shoved a chair into the tight space between General Heusinger and Colonel Brandt near the center. Hitler was already talking again. Stauffenberg squeezed past Colonel Brandt into his chair, whispering apologies, and deposited the briefcase at his feet. His arm still under the table, he glanced at his watch.

Twenty minutes.

One of Hitler's aides spread out a map and used a pointer to reference places as the Führer mentioned them. Stauffenberg made a point of listening intently. No one could see his toes tapping urgently inside his boots. He checked his watch again.

Thirteen minutes.

Hitler kept talking and the colonel kept his eyes on him. When the advisors finally began to ask questions and a discussion ensued, he let himself glance at the watch face again.

Four minutes.

He turned to Colonel Brandt. "So sorry, I need to——," he whispered.

Brandt shot him a look of irritation but stood up so he could get out. When Stauffenberg had slipped past, he scooted his chair back in, ramming his knee against the sturdy case the other colonel had left under the table. Scowling down at it, he rubbed his knee and shoved the case out of his way on the other side of the wide table leg.

Stauffenberg looked straight ahead as he stepped out of the building.

"Sir?" said the surprised commandant.

"I need to make a telephone call to Berlin."

"That way, sir."

Stauffenberg walked briskly toward the building the commandant pointed out. But he did not go in. Without breaking his gait he passed the building and went straight to the clearing where all the staff cars were parked, the drivers waiting with engines switched off.

"Everything all right, sir?" his driver said, scrambling to open the door for the colonel.

He slid into the back seat. "To the airport, corporal."

The corporal had turned the starter and put the vehicle into gear when a nearby blast rattled the car. The driver jerked his head to see a cloud of smoke and concrete dust roll up from the complex into the trees. "Sir!," he cried.

"I said, to the airport, corporal! Step on it!"

The driver hit the gas and sent the car careening toward the exit road. Bracing himself in the back seat, the war hero exhaled with a rush. At last, Hitler is dead!

Twenty-four hours later at Tegel Prison in Berlin, several prisoners and a guard huddled over a radio the guard had smuggled into the infirmary. The prisoners had been praying together in their sick beds, led by their fellow, a broad-shouldered man with thinning hair and rimless glasses. But when a foreign news dispatch came over the radio, they instantly fell silent and turned it up as loud as they dared.

"An attempt has been made on the life of Adolf Hitler," came the British-accented voice of a male announcer. "Reports indicate that a bomb was detonated at a meeting of top aides at the Reich's *Wolfsschanze* field headquarters in Rastenburg. A stenographer and three officers were killed, and the Führer received injuries to one arm but is very much alive. In an overnight radio broadcast, Hitler denounced his attackers as a 'criminal clique of reactionary officers,' and congratulated the German people on their Führer's providential escape, assuring them that the armed forces are unshaken in their loyalty——."

The guard snapped off the radio. The prayer leader's face had gone white, but he smiled at each of the sick patients in turn. "In God's time, brothers," he said, gently resting a hand on one man's shoulder and then another. "'God is our refuge and strength, a very present help in trouble,'" he quoted.

"What would we do without you, Pastor Bonhoeffer?" said one man, rising on his elbows.

"Probably get more sleep!" retorted the pastor, the corners of his blue eyes crinkling in a smile. "I'll come again as soon as I can. Until then, I will remember you in my prayers."

He held the gaze of the guard as he was escorted out. As soon as they reached the staircase, Corporal Knobloch grabbed his elbow and whispered, "He is invincible, Dietrich!"

Dietrich Bonhoeffer looked at his feet as he climbed the metal stairs. Even in prison he buffed his shoes everyday, but without a supply of polish it was impossible to cover the scuffs. "Not invincible," he murmured.

"I am sorry for your friends," the guard continued under his breath, glancing behind him as they entered the cellblock. "You are all in the worst danger now."

Dietrich leaned against the wall, arms folded, as the guard unlocked the heavy cell door. "You assume that since I was arrested under suspicion of being a conspirator, I must know something about this plot. But I've been incarcerated here for over a year. What could I have to do with this?"

The guard went into the cell with him and shut the door hastily. A barricaded window on the outside wall illuminated the small room. It held a narrow bed, where a wool blanket lay neatly folded at the foot of the mattress, and a wooden desk, marked with etchings by previous occupants and stacked with papers and books.

Dietrich took the stool at the desk and stretched out his long legs. Knobloch leaned against the desk.

"You and I both know your current status makes no difference," the guard said quietly. "They will draw this conclusion, with or without evidence. And such a bold plot—a lot of people must have been involved, and someone is bound to talk. Surely they will eventually discover the connection to you."

Dietrich pulled off his glasses and rubbed at his temples. "It does appear my fate has been sealed," he said finally. "I can only imagine what the family is going through right now. Have they told Hans in prison? Christine must be beside herself. And poor Klaus and Eberhard! Dear God, have mercy."

"I'll see if I can find out anything," Knobloch promised. "And I was able to meet Maria for a few moments this morning. She is going to sneak one of the books you asked for into your next laundry delivery. And she gave me this." He pulled a thin envelope from an inside pocket.

Dietrich snatched up the letter and ran his fingers across the smooth paper. "God bless you, Knobloch!"

"I'm sorry you will not be able to marry that beautiful young woman."

The prisoner looked him in the eye. "Lord willing, perhaps after the war."

Knobloch dropped his gaze to the floor. "Lord willing. Yes." He moved toward the door, but then turned back. "Dietrich, I know as a German you care about the future of our country. But, as a theologian, do you believe God wants Hitler dead?"

Dietrich was quiet. He remembered Hitler's speeches as he rallied the people to war. "We will not allow others to harm us," Hitler had shouted to the crowds. "Germany is strong in spirit, God—we will not let you go. Now bless us! Bless our liberty!" The people had cheered. Dietrich shuddered at the Führer's claim of divine blessing, and the blind dedication of the people who followed him even as he began to march Jews off to the death camps.

"I believe God wants justice for the Jewish people," he answered.

"But is that justice to come through you? Through a pastor?"

Dietrich leaned forward, his shoulders relaxed. "As a pastor, it is my duty to comfort the victims of a man who drives down a busy street like a maniac. Is it therefore not also my duty to try to stop that man?"

"But how can you know?" the guard pressed on.

Dietrich shook his head. "I cannot know. The Holy Scriptures do not say, 'Dietrich, stop Hitler at any cost.' But I am convinced in my heart that under these circumstances, it is the only just action." He paused, and then continued, his voice steady. "Murder is wrong, for Hitler and for me. But his actions kill millions of people and my actions may kill one and save millions of others. So I obey, acknowledging that there will be divine consequences to my actions."

They were silent. Then Knobloch glanced at the unopened letter still in Dietrich's hand, knuckles white from gripping the precious object. He roused himself abruptly. "I'll leave you to your reading. *Guten nacht*." He tipped his gray cap.

Dietrich gave him a grateful smile. "Good night, my friend."

Knobloch's key was still turning in the lock as the prisoner tore open the envelope. Tears trickled freely as he read it once, twice, three times, memorizing his fiancée's words and the elegant shape of her handwriting on the page. These letters were his only way of getting to know her, since his arrest had come only weeks after their engagement. Each letter impressed him with her intelligence and bravery.

When he finished, he wiped his eyes and cleaned his glasses against his shirt. Tenderly, he refolded the letter and placed it with the others inside the back cover of one of his books.

"Knobloch is right," he told himself. "Unless God intervenes, I probably don't have much time now." He slipped off his jacket and spread it neatly on the bed, then rolled up his shirtsleeves. As he reached for his pen and the stack of paper already covered with his writing, his mind quickly refocused on the last few points he had jotted in the book he was writing.

He called it simply "Ethics," and he believed it was the most important thing he had written. His other books talked about the tendency of the church to pursue "cheap grace." He meant that some people casually accept God's forgiveness without carefully considering the real cost of being a disciple of Jesus. If Christians truly followed Christ to the cross, he believed, they would stop living for themselves and instead give themselves for others. Now that he was in prison for trying to stop the Nazis, he had a lot more he wanted to write about how Christians could make the best decisions about living in a terribly broken world.

"How long have I been working on this project?" he asked himself. It had been several years at least. Back then, Hitler had already declared war on more than one country and determined to wipe out the Jewish people. As a Lutheran pastor, Dietrich was appalled that the church was putting their German nationality before their Christian duty and giving in to the Führer's demands to dismiss all Jewish pastors. Dietrich had helped start a secret seminary at Finkenwalde to train leaders for their "Confessing Church," one which denied Hitler the right to interfere with church decisions.

One of his students at the seminary was a young man named Eberhard Bethge, who had become a good friend. They often talked of God's grace and what it demanded of them while Hitler was thrusting their nation into war. Dietrich remembered one time when he and Eberhard sat outside a café near Memel. The sun had shone from a cloudless sky.

"It's hard to believe we can be at war on such a beautiful day," Eberhard had said.

"The submarines and minesweepers we passed on the ferry are a terrible enough reminder."

"Yes, if only——." Eberhard's words were cut short by the German anthem booming from a streetside speaker.

"Hitler is victorious in France!" came the voice of an announcer. "France has surrendered to Germany!"

Dietrich and Eberhard stared at each other in dismay. Instantly, their quiet coffee break was broken by the rush of café customers and passing pedestrians in joint salute on the sidewalk, belting out the national anthem.

Dietrich jumped up from his chair and thrust out his hand in salute.

"What are you doing?" Eberhard cried.

But Dietrich yanked Eberhard to his feet. "Are you insane? Raise your arm!" he shouted back.

Stunned, Eberhard did as his friend insisted.

The crowd grew boisterous as people climbed on chairs, still chanting. Dietrich lowered his arm, dropped enough money to the table to cover their coffees, and pulled Eberhard away. They walked briskly down the street.

"Why did you salute Hitler?" Eberhard demanded when they had cleared the crowd.

"If we hadn't done it, they would have noticed," Dietrich replied evenly. "I will risk myself for the resistance efforts, but not for a meaningless salute. It was just moral camouflage, Eberhard."

Eberhard stopped walking. "You have changed, Dietrich."

"How do you mean?"

"You and your family were pacifists. When I was your student, we had heated discussions about the value of passive resistance. You were planning on meeting with Mahatma Gandhi to learn about it from him, remember? And now you're telling me about organized resistance efforts and calling your salute 'moral camouflage'?"

"My ethics are a work in progress."

"Explain."

The pastor was quiet for a moment, gazing at the trees along the water and wriggling his hands in the pockets of his trousers. Then he said, "None of us is released from the responsibility of being a Christian. Not even—perhaps especially—in times of war and great suffering." He turned to look his friend in the eye. "I believe we should no longer ask simply what is right for us to do. We must ask what the will of God is."

"What is the will of God, then?" Eberhard's eyes as he held his friend's gaze were bright with earnestness.

"The will of God is for me to try to save others, even at great personal cost to myself." Dietrich took a deep breath and let it out slowly. "The reality is not a simple choice between right and wrong, Eberhard. The reality is that we live in a crooked and deformed world. None of our options is perfect. I'm learning to rely on grace, but—well, grace is costly."

"Costly grace," Eberhard murmured as they began to walk on.

It was a cost Dietrich's family knew all too well, now that he and Hans were in prison. His family were leaders of the community, people who had a lot to give and a lot to lose. Dietrich's father was a famous professor, his mother the granddaughter of a count. One older brother was a physicist and another was a lawyer, and two of his sisters had married lawyers. His sister Christine's husband Hans was the personal assistant of Germany's Minister of Justice—at least, he was before his arrest.

Dietrich had surprised them all by deciding to become a pastor. They thought he had chosen a quiet, boring life. But they had willingly joined him in discussions of Christian doctrine. They were all interested in what God had in store for the future of their country.

One family discussion stood out in his memory as he bent over the stack of pages on his desk. He had been visiting Christine and Hans. A number of family members were there in the spacious parlor—including Eberhard, who had recently proposed to Dietrich's niece. They were talking quietly in groups of two and three, enjoying each other's company and the warm flickers of the fireplace. The subject soon turned to Hitler, as it often did.

"You're willing to rouse the church to stand up to his religious policies, Dietrich. So why shouldn't the government resist his political ones? Do you not agree that Hitler's tyranny on all counts must be stopped?"

The questions came from Hans. When Hans smiled, he had a boyish twinkle in his eyes, but these days his face was almost always drawn and serious. Everyone's was.

The parlor fell silent. Everyone leaned forward in their sofas and arm chairs, curious to hear how the family theologian would reply.

Dietrich picked up his drink from the top of the piano, where he had been playing softly while they talked. He was the family musician, too, and they always asked him to play whenever they gathered in one of their homes.

"Even a tyrant is ordained to that position by God," he answered. He took a sip of his drink, and the room was so silent they could all hear the ice clinking against his glass.

Christine rose from the sofa closest to the fireplace and came over to the piano. "Yes, brother, but God uses instruments, does he not?"

"True."

"And those who live by the sword, die by the sword," Hans insisted.

"You're right, of course," Dietrich nodded, "but—doesn't that go for conspirators as well as tyrants?"

Hans frowned and moved closer to the fire, and Dietrich went back to playing Schubert. But when dinner was announced and the family straggled toward the dining room, he found himself in the corner with his brother-in-law, out of earshot of the rest.

"The overthrow of Hitler is a dangerous commitment," Dietrich said softly. "Are you sure you want to be involved? Think of my sister."

"I am!" Hans's voice rose, his words coming fast. "How often does this family sit late into the evening decrying the evils of this regime? What we need now is someone who will do something about it!" He caught himself and began again more slowly. "It's only a matter of time before you are conscripted for military duty again. Are you going to flee to America?"

Dietrich shook his head. "My friends at Union Seminary in New York continue to beg me, but I can't go back there now. What right would I have to lead the church in a free Germany if I wasn't willing to serve her in distress?"

Hans lowered his voice. "There is another option besides America."

"Hans——."

"I can get you a position with me at Military Intelligence."

"What use is a theologian to Military Intelligence?"

"Our resistance movement is growing. There are quite a few of us, and at the highest levels."

Dietrich raised a hand. "You shouldn't be telling me this. I don't understand how I could——."

"You have ecumenical connections outside of Germany. We could use those connections to negotiate with the Allies for a favorable truce once Hitler is out of the way."

Dietrich stared openly at him. "You want me to become a spy for the Reich?"

"Military Intelligence would just be your cover," Hans insisted. "You'd be a double agent for the resistance."

"I'm a pastor, Hans, a——a professor of theology! I'm not a spy!"

Hans grabbed his shoulder. "Would you rather be one of Hitler's soldiers dying on a God-forsaken front? Dietrich, I do not want God or history to know Hans von Dohnanyi as one who sat by while a madman killed millions of people. Is that how you want to be remembered?"

Dietrich took off his glasses and kneaded his temple. "If I were to do this," he realized silently, "I must accept that I am no longer qualified to be a pastor. How can a pastor have blood on his hands? But don't the pastors who are refusing to do something already have the blood of the Jews on their hands?"

Hans watched Dietrich's face as he grappled with himself. "All I ask is that you give this more thought," he said gently. "In the Justice Office, I read first-hand reports of Hitler's atrocities. I have been cataloging these in a Chronicle of Shame. I'll show it to you! And when you see it, you will understand. The crimes against the Jews will continue to fill this book, so long as good people sit back and do nothing."

From the doorway to the dining room, Eberhard glanced over at them, and then went inside, frowning.

"Stay after, and I will show you the book," Hans whispered. "By the end of the year, you could be working for us."

Dietrich sighed. "Soon you'll have the whole family involved! I take it Eberhard is not yet sure of this?"

"None of us are sure, Dietrich," Hans replied, spreading his hands. "But while we seek certainty for ourselves, people are being murdered. The time for debating is over."

Over. What a final word, Dietrich thought now, staring at the notes he had written. The resistance was over—it had failed to stop Hitler. Life as his family had known it was over—how many of them had already been implicated as conspirators? Hans was already in prison, and sick, last Dietrich had heard. Had they found his Chronicle of Shame, the book that had finally convinced Dietrich to become a double agent and help sneak hundreds of Jews out of Germany? Had the others been arrested?

And yet, he realized, his faith was not over. In fact, the failure of the resistance and the loss of his family had taught him more about that other word, the important one. The word *costly*.

He believed even more strongly now in costly grace, in completely giving himself to Christ in response to Christ's gift of life to him. Before his arrest, he had ministered to students and church members. Now he ministered in prison. He prayed with condemned men before their executions, read to inmates in the infirmary, and counseled guards who came to him with questions. It had cost him his freedom, but he had done what he thought was right, and even gained new opportunities to serve. "How many pastors get the chance to serve prisoners every day as one of them?" Dietrich asked himself again. "I am here for some purpose, and only hope I may fulfill it."

He was still thinking about these things while he unfolded the scratchy blanket over his legs in bed, after the guards had called, "Lights out!," and shut off the electric. He used the dark hours to sort his thoughts and pray so he could be ready to write again when the first rays of early light slanted through the iron window bars in the morning.

For several months he worked this way. When he was in his cell, he wrote his book. When he was in the exercise yard, the group showers, the infirmary, or the library, he taught and prayed with his fellow prisoners and guards. The guards helped him smuggle secret messages to his family so he could encourage them, too.

More than once, he was taken to the interrogator for questioning. Each time he wondered if they had found Hans' hidden papers, the ones that could prove he was part of the conspiracy against Hitler.

And one day in October, they did. It was Corporal Knobloch who told him, slipping into his cell to deliver the news in private.

"But if they have found the papers," said Dietrich, turning wide eyes to the guard, "that means——."

"Yes." Knobloch cleared his throat. "I am sorry to tell you your brother Klaus was arrested yesterday. It's only a matter of time before they have rounded up the others. And I doubt the prison officials will continue to make concessions for Hans' illness."

"Oh, what my parents must be going through!" Dietrich dropped his head onto his arms, folded across the desk.

"Listen," the guard continued. "They are moving you to the Reich Central Security Office so the Gestapo can question you on their own terms. But if we move quickly, we still may be able to execute our escape plan. I've made all the arrangements. I just need to——."

"No," said Dietrich, turning to him again. "Before this, there was a possibility, but now, now it is too dangerous. What would they do to Klaus or Hans if I disappeared? And my parents, my sisters, Maria! They might go after them looking for me. I cannot put them in more danger than they already are."

"But Dietrich!"

He raised a hand with a sharp "No!" But then he stood and stretched out his hand to the guard. "You went to great risk for me, and I have nothing but gratitude. You have been a good friend, an unexpected one in this place. Thank you, for everything."

"No, no. Can you ever forgive me for being part of this?" The guard gestured at the close cement walls and the heavy wooden door that blocked Dietrich from his past and his future.

"Of course. We all have our roles to play."

"But how can God—will God," Knobloch went on with a rush, "forgive a man for trying to serve his country and becoming a tool of injustice? Tell me! What will he say to me, the jailer of his servant Bonhoeffer?"

"I forgive you, my friend," Dietrich said gently. "As for God, you must plead for his mercy, as must I. Before him, you and I are equal in our crimes. Only his mercy will cover us both."

They were quiet, and then Knobloch said with a sad smile, "Once a pastor, always a pastor, even in here!" The smile faded. "They could move you at any time. I may have few more opportunities to help you. What can I do?"

Dietrich sat down again and reached for his pen. "Go to my sister and tell her we have abandoned the escape plan. And give me a few minutes to write some letters. I doubt I will be able to communicate with anyone once I reach the Central Security Office."

"I'll come back in an hour then," he promised. And with a quick glance into the corridor, he slipped out again.

Within days, Dietrich was moved to the underground prison at the Central Security Office. For four months, he was interrogated by the Gestapo. But as the days passed, the Allied Forces drew closer and closer to Germany. Air raids destroyed sections of the Security Office. Hitler ordered the "political prisoners" sent to the concentration camp at Buchenwald. So Dietrich was moved once again, on a bitter February day.

During the weeks at Buchenwald, he was quick to make friends, and his ministry continued as it had at Tegel. He also had long conversations through the wall with the man in the cell next to his, a Catholic politician named Hermann Pünder who shared his concern about the future of the church after the war. And in the washroom, he met a captured British agent named Payne Best, who kept everyone's spirits up with a ready supply of jokes.

Easter dawned in early April, and with it came cannon fire, shaking the basement cells.

"It's the Allies!" Payne shouted from his cell. "And on Easter, no less. Guess they want to put some resurrection fear into the Germans, like the Roman soldiers fainting at the open tomb!"

"Dietrich," came Hermann's voice through the wall. "What do you think this means?"

Dietrich put his lips to the wall. "Seems there are only two options. Either the Nazis will execute us, or the Allies will rescue us."

"But the Nazis have no intention of letting their prisoners be rescued," he thought.

Three nights later, they were roused from sleep and told to pack their possessions quickly. Dietrich's group was herded onto a truck fueled by a wood-burning generator. It was smoky and so packed with firewood that the prisoners had to squeeze together. Every bump on the road threw them into each other's laps.

"Where do you suppose they're taking us?" asked Payne.

"Can you see anything yet, Kokorin?" Dietrich called to a young man pressed against the door. Wasily Kokorin was a Russian agent, and Payne had laughingly introduced him to Dietrich as "the atheist." During their time at Buchenwald, Dietrich had taken every opportunity to talk to him about Christianity, and the young man had willingly taught him some Russian.

Kokorin had one eye to a small hole in the door, their only source of fresh air in the truck. "Still too dark," he said. But a few minutes later, he said, "Getting lighter." And then after another delay, he twisted away from the hole and faced the others with a grim set of his lips. "I've seen a sign. We're headed to Flossenbürg."

No one replied. They were all thinking the same thing: the extermination camp.

But the truck didn't turn toward Flossenbürg. Instead, it continued south, and after a few hours they stopped and the doors were flung open. They were led into the cells of a small courthouse and held there for several days. The guards wouldn't answer their questions.

Then, during the night, they were again loaded onto the smoke-filled truck and sent wheezing and rumbling toward another unknown destination. Rain drummed on the roof all morning, and the truck kept skidding on the wet roads, knocking together the prisoners inside. After one such episode, the tires slipping and the driver jerking the wheel, the truck came to a sudden stop and the engine cut out. The prisoners banged on the sides of the truck until the back door opened.

"The steering is broken," announced one of the guards. "Get out and stretch your legs while we wait, but no funny business. We're all armed."

After so many hours breathing in the thick wood smoke, Dietrich didn't mind standing in the fine drizzle. The air was cold and wet, but also fresh. He drew it deep into his lungs.

The wait was short. An old bus soon lumbered around the bend, and the guards commandeered it and herded the prisoners on board. This time, they didn't stop until they reached the village of Schönberg. The bus pulled up in front of a school clearly being used as another prison. As they went up the stairs, they could hear other prisoners behind locked doors. Dietrich and his friends were locked into a large classroom on an upper floor.

"What's this?" cried Payne with a laugh, dumping his bag at his feet. "Real beds with quilts? Huge windows? Electricity? One of you guys forget to tell me you're the king or something?"

"I get the bed by the window!" Kokorin shouted and threw his knapsack across the room to stake his claim.

Dietrich turned to Hermann with a grin. "Doesn't take much to please them, does it?"

The grown and somber prisoners suddenly became kids at recess, laughing and teasing each other. Each claimed a bed, and when Dietrich produced the stub of a pencil from his luggage, they took turns writing their names on the walls above their pillows. Soon they were unpacking and comparing their few belongings. Kokorin had a deck of cards. Dietrich had a few books. Payne had an electric razor.

"Pass it around so everyone can shave, and I'll read aloud!" Dietrich suggested.

So they spent the rest of that day and all of the following one in pleasant companionship. The rain cleared up and warm yellow sunshine, shut away from them for months, now streamed into the room. Dietrich sat for hours in a window, sunning himself, and practiced speaking Russian with Kokorin. Later, the guards delivered a mountain of potato salad, prepared for them by a woman in the village. They savored every bite.

The next day was Sunday, and Hermann rose with an idea. "Perhaps Pastor Bonhoeffer would lead us in a service," he suggested. "It is the first Sunday after Easter and likely our last. An appropriate action, wouldn't you say, Dietrich?"

"But rather difficult for a Lutheran clergyman," said Dietrich with his gentle smile. "You're Catholic, Hermann. Half of these men are. And young Kokorin here is an atheist!"

"Don't mind me," Kokorin shrugged. "It would be something to take our minds off anyway."

"Yes, please do, Bonhoeffer," Payne agreed.

"All right then," said Dietrich. He still had his Bible among his things, and got it out now.

The men settled themselves on the sides of the beds. Hermann brushed the sleeves of his coat with his hands, shook it, and then put it on. Payne grinned at his attempt to clean up for church.

Dietrich took off his glasses and polished them carefully before turning the pages of his Bible. "The Old Testament reading for the first Sunday after Easter is Isaiah chapter 53. 'With his wounds we are healed,'" he read. He flipped toward the back of his Bible. "And the New Testament reading is from the first epistle of Peter, the first chapter: 'Blessed be the God and Father of our Lord Jesus Christ! By his great mercy we have been born anew to a living hope through the resurrection of Jesus Christ from the dead.'"

"Let us pray," he said, and they bowed their heads. He led them through the prayers from his Lutheran prayer book that he knew by heart, remembering with joy the hundreds of services he had led after his time at seminary. Then he explained the texts he had read, and invited them to talk about the things they had learned in captivity.

When Dietrich closed the service, Hermann stood. "Thank you! I wish we could smuggle you into the other rooms to do the same for all the prisoners! It would do them good."

But the door rattled then, and a key turned in the lock. Two guards stood in the doorway. "Prisoner Bonhoeffer," said one. "You are to come with us. Collect your things."

The men looked from Dietrich to each other, then dropped their gazes in frustrated sorrow.

All of Dietrich's things were in his bag except his Bible. He tucked it inside, but drew another book out. With the pencil stub, he wrote his name in three places and handed it to Hermann. "Read it, if you'd like," he said, "and then, if you ever get out of here, see it gets back to my family, would you?"

"Of course, Dietrich!" Hermann accepted the book like it was a land grant from the king.

Dietrich turned to Payne. "If you make it back to England, remember me to the bishop of Chichester. He was a good friend."

"Right. Certainly." Payne cleared his throat. "Guess this is the end, Bonhoeffer."

Dietrich smiled. "This is the end of many things—but for me, it's the beginning of life."

"God bless you!" was all Payne could say. He reached for a final handshake, and every man in the room lined up to do the same.

The guards locked the door behind them, and the prisoners could hear calls of "God bless you, Pastor Bonhoeffer!" coming from the other classrooms. They crowded around the windows to catch a last glimpse of Dietrich as he was led out of the building and into a waiting truck. As soon as the doors were latched, the engine started up with a cough. Dietrich's friends watched with heavy hearts as the truck disappeared into the haze of green hills in the direction of Flossenbürg.

Dietrich Bonhoeffer was hanged at the Flossenbürg concentration camp on Monday, April 9, 1945. Three weeks later, on April 30, Adolf Hitler committed suicide, and Germany's surrender to the Allies led to the end of World War II. But by then, Dietrich's brothers-in-law Hans von Dohnanyi and Rüdiger Schleicher and his brother Klaus had also been executed, leaving the Bonhoeffer family deeply bereft.

Eberhard Bethge survived imprisonment and saw to it that Dietrich's book Ethics was published. He also collected the letters he and others had received from his dearest friend and published them later as Letters and Papers from Prison. Those books and his Cost of Discipleship are among the most moving and influential of Bonhoeffer's writings. He wrote more during his months at Tegel Prison than any other period of his life.

Bonhoeffer's beloved fiancée Maria von Wedemeyer became a mathematician. She eventually married, had two children, and lived most of her life in the United States. She died in 1977.

Big Moments in Modern Christianity

ALL THROUGH THE history of the church, Christians have experienced important moments that changed the way they related to one another—within one local church, one denomination, or one region— or the way they related to the world. Let's look at a few of these moments from the modern era.

THE PENTECOSTAL MOVEMENT

In 1906, one of the most influential Evangelical movements of modern Christianity held a meeting in Los Angeles, California, and experienced a revival known today as the *Azusa Street Revival*. This *Pentecostal* movement spread throughout the world. What began in a California warehouse soon resulted in new denominations and new movements, such as the *Charismatic Movement* (1960s). By the year 2000 there were over 500 million Pentecostal and Charismatic Christians worldwide!

In their earliest years, Pentecostals generally came from other Christian traditions, such as Methodist and Holiness. One of the most important figures for the movement was Charles Fox Parham (1873-1929), a former Methodist who believed the church was entering a new age foretold by the Old Testament prophet Joel called "the latter rain." He became an evangelist, preaching the need for an "added blessing" or baptism in the Holy Spirit, intended to take the Christian into higher, holier living. This baptism was marked by the act of speaking in tongues (as mentioned in Acts 2), and might include prophesying or healing. One of Parham's students, William Seymour, the son of a former slave, began holding meetings in California. At the Azusa Street revival in 1906, people began seeking out the Pentecostal blessing, and the movement quickly picked up momentum.

Pentecostals have been very effective in their mission works and quick to communicate via modern forms of technology like radio, television, and the internet. And unlike many other church groups, black, white, and Hispanic Christians often worship together in Pentecostal meetings. But their beliefs about miracles and spiritual gifts have always met with controversy. Many Evangelicals from other Protestant traditions (such as Reformed, Presbyterian, and Lutheran) continue to question the legitimacy of interpreting the Bible the way they do.

THE FUNDAMENTALIST AND MODERNIST CONTROVERSY
Toward the end of the 1800s, people generally looked to human reason to understand the universe and were suspicious of religious authorities. These modernists thought the world would improve if they focused on science and education instead of Scriptural teaching. Many Protestants found that their credibility as Christians was challenged by the rise of two big modernist concepts, *naturalism* and *biblical higher criticism*.

The first concept, *naturalism*, is the rejection of divine and supernatural influence over the natural world. The big example of this is Charles Darwin's theory of evolution, which allows for the creation and development of life on earth without the need for a God. The second concept, *biblical higher criticism*, examines the texts of the Bible without necessarily assuming its divine authority. Evangelicals historically insisted that the Bible was without error, but others saw it as just another ancient text that should be treated like any other human book.

Wanting to be honest, some Christians decided to take these ideas seriously and see what answers their faith offered in response. They tried to find a middle ground between traditional Christian doctrines and the new modern understanding of the world. They did not believe that Christianity and evolution, or Christianity and higher criticism, were contradictory. God, they concluded, could have just guided evolution, so even if naturalism was true, it didn't leave out God. And they saw the point of the Bible as being a place to meet Christ, not a place to look for facts that might or might not be in error.

Some Christians ultimately rejected evolution and any view of the Bible that allowed for some definition of "error" in Scripture. In America, these Evangelicals became known as *Fundamentalists*. In the early years of the modern period, this term implied someone who holds to the fundamental beliefs of Christianity, including the historical reality of miracles in Scripture, the virgin birth, the resurrection, and the second coming of Christ.

Representative of the struggle between fundamentalism and modernism at this time was the now-famous *Scopes Monkey Trial*. In 1925, in Dayton, Tennessee, John T. Scopes was charged for violating a state law that forbade the teaching of evolution—but what ended up on trial was the validity of the creation account in Genesis 1. William Jennings Bryan led the prosecution, and Clarence Darrow the defense, and the case received worldwide attention. Scopes was found guilty of breaking the law, but the law was repealed in 1967.

Fundamentalists continued to battle over what they saw as the greatest threat to Christianity. The Moody Bible Institute in Chicago became a key college for promoting fundamentalist beliefs. Other schools ended up splitting over these issues. Princeton Theological Seminary, for example, which was originally seen as a fortress against modernism, found itself in a controversy over these issues in the early 1900s. Several professors, including J. Gresham Machen (1881-1937), split from Princeton in 1929 to form Westminster Theological Seminary in Philadelphia for the training of ministers in the Reformed and Presbyterian denominations.

THE NEW EVANGELICALS

While fundamentalists pressed on in their fight against modernism, they found themselves losing ground in denominations and schools across the country. It didn't bother some of them that they were not welcomed among America's intellectuals. But others began calling themselves *neo* (or new) Evangelicals. Rather than separate from the world, the neo-Evangelicals believed it was important to be active in culture, education, social concerns, and especially evangelism. Many of them, like J. Elwin Wright (1890-1972), Carl F.H. Henry (1913-2003), and Harold Ockenga (1905-1985), put their support behind a new Evangelical organization to promote these goals, called the *National Association of Evangelicals* (1942). Since then, this organization has been a prominent voice for Evangelicals in America.

And continuing this work, Evangelicals formed other organizations, like the *Evangelical Theological Society* (1949), to engage in academic discussion. Schools such as Trinity Evangelical Divinity School and Wheaton College took the lead in training new leaders. Billy Graham, possibly the most famous Evangelical, started the influential magazine *Christianity Today* in 1956, and began to broadcast his evangelism tours to television sets across the world.

Today, Evangelicalism is known worldwide and continues to be a powerful force for social change and political influence. The new

Evangelicals—including some members of a movement currently known as the *Emerging Church*—are diverse in their beliefs and are engaging new issues, but they still emphasize the gospel of Christ as the center of their teaching. So the story of Evangelicalism is still being written!

THE VATICAN COUNCILS AND
PROTESTANT-CATHOLIC DIALOGUE

Protestants weren't the only ones to face the challenges of modernity. The rise of the French Enlightenment and the French Revolution of 1789 specifically challenged the authority of the Roman Catholic Church. The *First Vatican Council* (1869-1870) made it clear that Catholic Christianity was opposed to the ideas of modernism. But a century later, Pope John XXIII saw the *Second Vatican Council* (1962-1965) as an opportunity to meet the challenges of the modern world. This time, the council did not reject modernism. It argued for the legitimacy of other Christian traditions, especially the Eastern Orthodox Church, and there were even non-voting representatives of Christians from other traditions, including Protestants. Many Catholics saw these conclusions as a necessary step for Catholic Christianity to survive in the ever-changing world, one that offered new approaches to missions. Others saw it as a compromise of the Church's traditional beliefs.

Protestants and Catholics have been at odds ever since Protestants were condemned by the Roman Church during the Reformation. But since Vatican II, some Protestants have discussed reuniting with the Catholic Church. Other Evangelical Protestants took Vatican II as one of many signs of a modernist and liberal victory, further widening the divide between Evangelical Protestants and Catholics. Evidence of this divide was clear in the 1990s, when American Evangelical theologians and Catholic theologians began discussing some kind of union of their respective groups—and a firestorm of debate broke out on both sides. In 2007, Pope Benedict XVI infuriated some Protestants and some Catholics when he declared that Vatican II was not an open door for Protestants as many believed. So the conclusions of the council remain a matter of debate today.

C.S. Lewis: All Worlds End Except Aslan's Own Country

OCTOBER 19, 1956. OXFORD, ENGLAND.

THE PROFESSOR CUT through the corner of the car park, his leather soles beating a rapid *thwick-thwack* on the pavement. The rhythm muffled as he turned again, this time making a beeline across the green in front of Wingfield-Morris Orthopaedic Hospital. The grass was still damp, and he kicked up a fine spray of dew that flecked his shoes with dark spots.

Though he was in a hurry, he couldn't help noticing the brilliant gold and red shrubs and the watery diamonds dangling from the tips of the leaves. "These misty mornings turn every cobweb on the hedge into a necklace of heavy dew," he thought. The sun was warm on his back and he was glad he had left his overcoat at his office. His wool suit was heavy enough for the unseasonable weather.

Several elderly residents were stationed around the patio, sunning themselves in their wheelchairs. One man looked up from arranging his brown lap blanket and gave him a polite nod. "Bit of a 'St. Luke's Summer' we're having, eh?" he said in a wheezy voice.

The professor tipped his hat. "It's been years since I heard that phrase! And, yes, the weather is a delight."

He reached the patio door as it swung open. He held it for the nurse who was coming out with a tray of little cups of pills and saying, "Oh, thank you very much." Outside, she glanced at him, then away, and then back at him, recognition dawning on her face.

"Excuse me, are you Mr. Lewis?"

He nodded agreeably, and began to step around her.

"Mr. C. S. Lewis?"

He let out a deep sigh. "Yes, but everyone just calls me Jack. I'm here to see a patient, Mrs. Joy Gresham."

"Oh, yes. I can show you to her room. Follow me." He held the door for her again and followed her inside, past the reception area and down a long corridor of patient rooms. "She's just this way," she said, and then hung back to fall into step beside him. She turned her head, eyes bright and cheeks growing rosy, and began to gush. "I have to say it's rather exciting to run into you, Mr. Lewis! I've just purchased your latest Narnian book, *The Last Battle*, for my son and daughter."

She bit her lip and gave him a sidelong glance. Would he think it rude of her to chat up a famous writer while he was visiting a sick friend?

But he gave her the patient smile of a man who is used to being recognized. "I was just telling a friend that too many people refer to it as the 'Narnia series.' It is good to meet someone who still believes in adjectives. I hope you enjoy the book."

"Thank you!" She stopped before a door near the end of the corridor and turned to him. "This is the room. But, Mr. Lewis, do you know what I believe?"

"What's that?"

"Supposedly the Narnian books are for children, but I believe they are a ruse to get adults to use their imaginations again."

"Oh, you do?" he said, chuckling, his hand on the doorknob. "I'd say it is rather more than that."

"What then?"

"I'll let you discover that. But you might want to ask yourself, what was it that Susan Pevensie lost?" He gave her a friendly nod and slipped into the room, letting the door click behind him.

"What happens to Susan?" said the wide-eyed nurse. But the blank door did not respond. "Oh, dear!" she murmured as she bustled away.

The light in the room wasn't bright but it glared harshly off the bare walls. Everything in the room was white—the floor, the walls, the cotton bed linens—except for the patient's black hair. It was spread out across the pillows, where she lay with one leg raised above the metal bedframe in a contraption of wires and pulleys.

As he came up beside her, her eyes flickered open and her pale lips curved into a weak smile. "Jack!"

He bent over her, careful to avoid the leg, and patted her cheek. "Hello, Joy. I hear you took a rather large fall."

Her body was still, but a spark of amusement flared in her eyes. "You Brits exaggerate everything. Where are my boys?"

"They're with Warnie. He was happy to run over and stay with them." He drew the one chair in the room close to the bed and sat down. "What happened?"

"The strangest thing." She tried to sit up, but immediately winced and leaned back against the pillows again. "Apparently Katharine Farrer felt an urgency to call me. She had a feeling as if something was terribly wrong with me, so she picked up the phone to call at just the same time as I was crossing the house and tripped over the phone wire."

"Just as it was ringing?"

"No, that's the strange part. It hadn't yet rung, so I wasn't attempting to answer it. But I tripped and felt my leg snap. Since I had knocked the phone off the hook at just the time Katharine's call came through, I could hear her on the line saying, 'Hello? Joy?' So I shouted out to her that I was hurt and she came right over to the house. The next thing I know, I'm on my way to the hospital in an ambulance."

Jack was quiet, his heavy brows bunched in concentration.

She flung both hands wide. "Well, are you going to say something or are you just going to sit there like a lump?"

He chuckled, the lines in his face deepening as he smiled. "I'm sorry! I was just thinking about the odd string of events that had to happen for you to arrive here safely."

"Exactly!" She slapped playfully at his hand and he took it into his. "I'm sure it's going to end up in one of your books someday. You know, back when I was an atheist, I would have discounted a story like this that a Christian told me as pure fiction. But now, I just think God's timing is peculiar—and wonderful."

"So it is. Well, what's the word on your leg?"

"They're running tests. I've been poked, prodded, and injected with who knows what—and they just did X-rays. I should have an answer soon."

"I'll wait with you then."

She smiled. "So you rushed over from Cambridge in a panic to see me? How very sweet."

He chuckled again. "Not in a panic."

"Oh, yes. I know you."

"I simply wanted to make sure my American wife is as tough as she claims to be."

"So now you're willing to acknowledge I'm your wife?"

He waved his free hand. "To this empty room, yes."

She rolled her eyes. "Don't you think it's time we announced our marriage, Jack? You visit me so often at home, people are starting to talk."

"Gossip is easier to deal with than the real problems that would come with a public announcement."

"You still believe that? I take it you haven't told the faculty or any of your friends? Not even Tolkien or the other Inklings?"

He shook his head vigorously. "Oh, no. Good ol' Tollers would never let me hear the end of it. We've already gone to blows over what I've written on marriage. He nearly made me swallow my pipe the last time we discussed the issue."

"Are you suggesting writers are temperamental?"

He laughed. "You are one, so I guess you'd know! No, Tollers is an idealist. He could never understand why I would marry an American divorcee to help her keep her sons here in England."

"But surely you realize other women think you are available." She was on a roll now, perked up by Jack's vibrant presence. She pointed toward the door. "I heard you talking to that nurse, for example. I'm sure she thinks you are an eligible bachelor."

He shrugged. "I didn't lead her to believe that. And anyway, she's too young to be interested in an old man like me."

"So you've forgotten about the woman who checked into a hotel pretending to be the wife of the famous Professor Lewis? She rang up a rather large bill in your name."

"I have not forgotten, but she's in prison now."

"What about that antique dealer, then? She's still bothering you."

He wiggled his eyebrows dramatically. "That woman is absolutely off her rocker! She actually believes that my books are love letters to her and that only she has the key."

"And she still sends you letters?"

"Which I put directly into the fire bin."

"Uh-huh." She laughed awkwardly, her pleasure blunted by pain. "See what I mean? You need a sign around your neck that says, 'Reserved for Joy.' That's what a proper marriage announcement in the newspaper is for."

A sharp rap sounded at the door. Jack let go of Joy's hand as a nurse in a peaked white cap leaned in. "Mrs. Gresham, the doctor is looking over the results of your X-rays. He'll be in shortly to discuss them."

"That's fine, thank you."

But the young woman didn't immediately excuse herself. She had recognized her patient's visitor. "Why, Mr. Lewis!" she said, delight spreading across her face. "I'm a big fan of your writing and thoroughly enjoyed your last radio broadcast. Tell me, can this really be the last book for Narnia?"

With a quick glance at Joy, he politely returned the nurse's smile. "Yes, miss, it certainly is."

"But I can hardly believe it!"

"I have it on fairly good authority."

She laughed. "Of course. Well, in that case, I do hope you'll start something new for your fans to look forward to." She bobbed her cap and ducked out the door again.

Jack turned back to Joy, who was making a face at him, eyebrows raised. "You see?" she said.

He shook his head. "You'd think someone who works in a hospital would be used to things coming to an end."

"People are really having trouble over this being the last of it, aren't they?"

"Yes." He shifted his weight in the hard chair. "I suppose it's understandable. We all hope that we can save Narnia. My character Jill says she wishes it could 'go on for ever and ever and ever.' But Narnia is not an end and my readers will need to see that. As Jewel reminds Jill, 'all worlds draw to an end, except Aslan's own country.' We should all find hope in that eternal land instead of looking for it elsewhere, including Narnia."

She rolled her eyes. "How depressing you are!"

"The odd thing is, people seem most concerned about Susan."

"Well, you leave us with very little about her."

He shrugged. "Her story no longer belongs in Narnia."

"Well, just be glad people love the series so much."

"I am. I just wish they wouldn't have printed the books on that horrible paper!"

"The complaints of writers!" She waved away his comment. "Here—help me with these pillows. I just abhor trying to talk to you from down here."

He helped her into a sitting position and adjusted the pillows to support her back.

"Speaking of writing," she went on, "How are your colleagues accepting *Bareface*—I mean, *Till We Have Faces*." She made quotation marks in the air with her fingers as she mentioned the title.

"I still want to call the book *Bareface* as well."

"Your publisher is ridiculous to think it sounds like a western. However, I do agree that something is missing—shouldn't my name be on the cover?"

"It's not enough that I dedicated it to you?" He grinned and leaned back into the chair again, trying a different position. "I was shown a review of it from last week's *Time and Tide*."

"You've been holding out on me! What did the reviewer say?"

"He called it 'satisfactory,' but he was not thrilled. Apparently, people do not see or appreciate the parallels to the experience of becoming a Christian, and how that strains our relationships with unbelievers."

"It's a re-telling of an ancient myth, Jack. That alone makes it complicated reading."

He laced his fingers together and put them behind his head. "I suppose myths are just difficult for people to understand, let alone my reasons for re-telling one in today's language. But I want people to understand that great truths can be found in literature, truths about God himself."

"Well, it seemed plain enough to Warnie and I the weekend we helped you finish it!"

"You and my brother are both writers. Maybe my language wasn't clear enough for other people."

For the first time since he had entered her room, her face grew serious. "I think there is more to it than that," she said. "See, in your version of the story, you made Psyche's palace invisible to everyone except her. She sees it as the most beautiful thing of all. But since her sister can't see it, she is unable to appreciate its true value. All she sees are rocks and stubble, so she concludes that Psyche has gone mad. It's just like what happens when a person converts to Christianity. That man or woman sees Christ as beautiful, but to the unbelieving family members who cannot see Christ, that person is just crazy."

He gazed at her intently. "Go on."

"Well, perhaps this helps explain why the critics don't appreciate the book the way you and I do. The message of the book is like the invisible palace. For people like us, former atheists, Christianity was once invisible. I mean, until I started reading your books, I believed only in atheism! But your writings revealed the beautiful palace of Christianity. Now that I see its beauty, a book that portrays this new way of seeing has great meaning to me. But for those who still deny God's existence, perhaps the message is lost."

"Yes, I suppose books cannot speak to all people the same way. We need many great books that reflect different aspects of God's truth so that there is something to touch every person from every background. The audience of the Narnian books is mostly children. Maybe *Till We Have Faces* is more for people with worldly academic backgrounds like you and me."

Her eyes twinkled again, despite the purple shadows beneath them. "Well, I think the book is great and I'm never wrong."

He laughed with her, and then leaned over the bed. "I'm still amazed that I can have such conversations with you. How wrong I was to think intellectual discussion was limited to my university colleagues! That's what I love about you, Joy."

"Love?" she repeated in a mocking voice. But a knock at the door interrupted her teasing, and she called out, "Come in."

A bearded doctor stepped into the room and glanced at Jack, who had come to his feet. "I didn't realize you had company, Mrs. Gresham. Would you prefer me to come back later?"

"Oh, no, you can speak plainly in front of Jack. Besides, he already knows I'm hopelessly clumsy."

He offered Jack a handshake. "I'm Joy's doctor. You must be Professor Lewis."

"A pleasure to meet you."

The doctor turned back to his patient and cleared his throat. "I've been looking over your X-rays. You've had problems with your back and legs before?"

She nodded. "My last doctor diagnosed it as rheumatism and fibrositis."

"Yes," he said, glancing down at his clipboard. "Well, Mrs. Gresham, there is no easy way to tell you this. Either your previous physician missed it, or past X-rays did not show it. The one we did today reveals significant spots on the bone." He paused. "I'm afraid it is cancer. The reason your leg broke so easily when you fell is because the cancer has eaten away the bone."

She sucked in a mouthful of air, too stunned to speak.

"And it is spreading," the doctor continued, eyes downcast. "It will take several operations to cut out all the cancerous cells."

Her eyes drifted to the pulley holding up her leg. "I see," she murmured.

"Do you have someone to take care of you?"

Jack stepped forward. "Me."

The doctor turned to him. "The operations will be very painful. She will need someone to keep an eye on her daily."

"I will see to it."

He looked at his patient, who nodded. "I couldn't ask for a better nurse than Jack," she said, scrounging up a joke. "I'll have to get him one of those cute white caps."

The doctor gave her a compassionate smile. "Very well. We'll be setting your leg in a cast shortly, and I'll be back later to discuss the cancer treatments. We'll need to begin those right away."

She was quiet.

"Do you have any questions for me at the moment?"

"No, thank you." She looked away.

"This is always difficult, Mrs. Gresham. But you should never lose hope of victory. I'll check in on you soon."

The door opened and then clicked again, shutting out the voices and buzzing noises in the corridor. Joy's eyes were closed. The silence was suddenly unbearable. Jack dashed out of the room, calling down the hallway to the doctor.

"Yes, Mr. Lewis?," he said, turning.

Jack shoved his trembling hands in his pockets. "How much time does she have?"

"It's hard to say."

"You must have some idea."

"These things are unpredictable. All I can say is this is a very bad case."

"But there is a possibility she'll pull out of this?"

The physician glanced away.

"Answer my question, doctor! What are her odds?"

The doctor sighed and put a hand on the professor's shoulder. "I'm sorry, Mr. Lewis. Experience tells me your friend does not have much time." He gave his shoulder a pat and moved on down the hallway.

Jack drew the antiseptic hospital air deep into his lungs. He stepped back into Joy's room, stopping just inside the door. Her eyes fixed on his ashen face.

"I'm going to die, aren't I, Jack?"

"We're all going to die, Joy. You shouldn't lose hope. We have no idea what will happen here."

"I don't believe you. You have the same look on your face as you did when you told me how your mother died of cancer when you were a boy."

"This is different."

"Oh?" She shot him an angry look. "Do I have cancer confused with some other disease?"

He took both of her hands in his and dropped to the chair again. His voice was quiet. "What I mean is, we know the healer of all diseases. We'll beg him to deliver you. And I will take care of you. You and the boys will move in with me at The Kilns."

"Oh, Jack, we talked about this a few minutes ago! People don't know we are married. What will they say if I move into your house? It wouldn't be proper."

"Then it is time to do the proper thing. Joy, I married you so you and the boys could stay in England. But now, just now, I realized that if something happened to you—." He choked back the lump in his throat. "Something unexpected has occurred. Over these months of talking about Christianity and literature, I have fallen in love with you! And you're right—we must tell everyone about our marriage."

She looked happy again. "Then let's have a church wedding!"

His face fell. "I long to give you that, now. But I don't see how it's possible. The Church of England does not consider divorce legitimate, even in your case of Bill's abuse. You are still his wife in their eyes."

"Your friend Bishop Carpenter wouldn't perform the ceremony?"

"I will ask him, but I doubt he will see it our way." He rubbed his forehead. "It seems to me that if a divorced person cannot remarry, then your marriage to Bill was never legitimate, since he was divorced when he married you! Therefore, you were never legitimately married, so the church shouldn't object to our marriage." He sighed. "It's the logical argument, but one I doubt they will accept. Theology is beautiful, but it sometimes makes living difficult."

She looked him in the eye. "So does cancer."

He shuddered at the word and forced himself to go on. "Perhaps grace will be given to us on both counts. You try to conquer the cancer, and I'll try to arrange a proper church wedding. Do we have a deal, Mrs. Lewis?"

Her face was as pale as the linens in her bed, but she smiled up at him from her pillows. "Yes, Professor. We do."

So Joy began the painful treatments to stop the cancer from spreading. Jack visited her in the hospital every day, and between class lectures at the university he helped his brother Warnie care for her two young sons. He also went to work trying to arrange a church wedding.

"You are already legally married," Bishop Carpenter said, after Jack had explained the reasons why he believed their situation should be considered an exception. "Why do you want a church wedding?"

"The Church of England considers marriage a sacrament, and Joy wants to receive the blessing of that sacrament before she dies. And she is dying. I just want to move her into my house and take care of her for as long as she has. But we want the church's blessing first."

"It is tricky biblically," the bishop replied after a moment. "However, I confess that I see your point. But Jack, you are a celebrity, and unfortunately that makes this even more difficult. If I made an allowance for you, I would soon have to do it for everyone, and most people do not understand the finer theological points the way you do."

"So you won't marry us?"

"I'm sorry, Jack. I agree with you, but in this cassock"—he fingered his black clerical robe—"I don't represent myself, but the Church."

Jack went back to thinking about his problem. But the situation quickly grew even more complicated. One afternoon when he had returned to his university office after a long morning of lecturing, a reporter knocked at his door. He was writing a story for London's *Daily Mail*, he told Jack, because he'd been contacted by an antique dealer who said she and Jack were getting married in London in a few days! Jack set the reporter straight, and the next day, the paper ran a story exposing the woman's lie. But he discovered that it didn't put an end to the rumors about him getting married— instead, people were speculating about who he was really engaged to marry.

"These are the geniuses who read my books?" he fumed. But he had to take some of the blame, since he had hidden the truth from even his closest friends. It was time to come clean. So he went to the newspaper office and paid to publish a notice: "A marriage has taken place between Professor C. S. Lewis, of Magdalene College Cambridge, and Mrs. Joy Gresham, now a patient in the Churchill Hospital, Oxford." Then he went home and began writing letters to his friends.

Joy soon finished the cancer treatments. But her condition was worse than before. The doctors gave permission for Jack to care for her at home, and he moved her and the boys into The Kilns, the old house where he and his brother lived. He set up a hospital bed in the sunniest room, where through the tall windows she could enjoy the snowfall and later the first green shoots of spring.

While the boys were at school, Jack sat with her and kept her company. He took her mind off the pain by discussing Christian doctrine and telling her about the literature classes he was teaching. He read her drafts of the articles he wrote, and chapters from some of their favorite books. But when she continued to grow weaker, he called in an old friend.

"His name is Peter Bide, Reverend Bide," he explained the morning of his friend's visit. He was tucking the blankets under her legs, his brother Warnie standing behind him with extra pillows.

"You two—I've never seen such bald, cardigan-clad nurse's aides!" she said between coughs. "Why is this Bide fellow coming?"

"I've asked him to pray over you," said Jack. "He's a former student of mine. He's prayed for many sick people in the past and God has listened to him. I'm hoping he'll listen to him now."

"Thank you, Jack, but I'm losing more bone marrow every day. I think God has made it clear what he plans to do."

"Rest, my dear," Jack insisted. "We should never lose hope."

"Where are my boys?"

"Playing chess in the parlor," said Warnie. "I'll keep David and Douglas occupied while Peter is here."

Warnie answered Peter's knock later and ushered him into Joy's room, where Jack rose to greet him. "Thank you so much for coming," Jack said, hand outstretched to his friend.

"Anything I can do, Jack. And hello, Joy—it is a pleasure to meet you."

She gave him a weak smile. "Hello, Reverend. Jack hopes you can perform a miracle."

"Can't say I'll perform one, but I can at least ask for one."

"Then you have my gratitude. They say I'm not long for this world. I should be saying goodbye to the Shadowlands."

"Oh yes, the place Jack writes of in *The Last Battle*. I've read it, along with nearly everyone else, I think!" He grinned. "Best I can figure, it seems to be some sort of reference to the connection between philosophy and the Bible. Always the professor, isn't he?"

"He never stops lecturing me!" She clutched her ribs with a grimace as her laughter spurred more coughing.

"Do you trust God?" asked Peter.

She nodded.

"Then let him decide whether you are leaving the Shadowlands."

"You're right, Reverend," she said. "What good is it for a former atheist to finally believe in God, but not in his ability to heal?"

Jack sat beside her as Peter put a hand on her head and began to pray. He asked God to take away her pain and heal her. He asked God to remove the cancer. He asked for a miracle.

Afterward, Warnie insisted that Peter stay for tea, and got the boys to help serve everyone chocolate biscuits. When it was time to leave, Jack walked his friend out to his car.

"Thanks again, Peter. It means a lot that you came all this way."

"I will continue to pray for her—and for you. I can't imagine what you're going through."

Jack leaned into the open car window and decided to ask Peter the same questions he had posed to Bishop Carpenter. When he finished, Peter started the engine and said, "It's a very serious thing you are asking, Jack. Let me think about it. In the meantime, you are all in my prayers."

They needed those prayers more than ever over the next few days. The pain became unbearable, and Joy was moved back to the hospital for another round of tests. Each day, the news from the doctors was worse than the day before. Jack spent every possible moment praying with Joy at her bedside.

One morning, Peter Bide appeared at the door of her room. "It seems we shouldn't waste any more time," he said. He gestured to the crisp bedsheet draped over Joy's legs. "And I see the bride is already dressed in white."

"You've decided to perform the ceremony?" Jack said.

"Yes. I understand why the bishop declined to do it, but I asked myself, 'Does God believe this is a real marriage?' The church recognizes and blesses civil marriages all the time. Any clergyman would expect you to remain a faithful husband to Joy. By law you are one, after all. Ultimately the only 'higher court' that matters in this case is God, so once I asked myself what he would do, that somehow finished the argument."

Joy forced the pain from her mind and managed a smile. "God bless you, Reverend!"

"I'll give you some time to prepare yourselves while I go down and pray in the hospital chapel. I'll be back at, say, eleven?"

"Thank you," Jack said, and clasped his friend's hand firmly.

When Peter returned, Jack was sitting beside Joy, tucking into her hair a flower he had snatched from a vase. Warnie had joined them, too. Peter took his place at the foot of her bed, and with the late-morning sun streaming golden through the narrow hospital window, he married Jack and Joy. It was the closest Joy could get to a real church wedding, and she was happy.

In April, the doctors told her there was nothing else they could do for her. "Death is approaching," her doctor said gently. "You should be where you are loved, not in a hospital." So they moved her back into Jack's house. Her pain was so severe that she could not walk, and Jack and Warnie had to carry her from room to room. They hired nurses to visit her at home and help with her medication.

Every day, Jack sat at her bedside as she gritted her teeth, and begged God to heal her. "If someone must have the pain, take it from her and give it to me," he prayed over and over.

And he kept writing. "Ink is the great cure for all human ills," he told himself. If a Christian had to face so much suffering and doubt, he might as well put it into a book that would speak about those things to someone else who needed to hear them.

And then something unexpected happened. Joy began to smile more often and wince less. Her spirits rose. When the phone rang, she reached to answer it without hesitating. But at the same time, Jack's legs began to ache and he had less energy than usual. They both went to the doctor for tests. And when Jack got the results from his tests, he went straight home to tell Joy.

She was sitting in her favorite chair, knitting, her cane on the floor beside her. It was all she needed to get around these days.

"What did the doctor say?" she demanded.

He drew the opposite chair closer. "It's amazing, Joy!"

"I can handle amazing." She put down her yarn and needles and looked at him expectantly.

"I have my own bone disease."

"What? Then why are you smiling?"

"The doctors say I have premature calcium loss. The intriguing thing is that while I am losing calcium in my bones, you are gaining it in yours."

She was quiet. "Jack, didn't you pray that you could take my pain?"

He nodded.

"This is about as strange as my tripping over the phone cord while Katharine was ringing through!" she said, eyebrows arched. "What are your treatment options?"

"There is no cure, but it's not life-threatening. For now, I have to take calcium tablets and wear a support belt round my waist. There will be medication for the pain. But if this is a bargain from God, I'm very thankful for it!"

She reached for his hand. "I don't know what to say about these odd events that keep cropping up in our life together, except that this God we believe in works in mysterious ways."

"I thought I was going to become a husband and a widower in the same day." He shook his head and leaned toward her. "But perhaps life in the Shadowlands will go on a bit longer."

"I'm grateful for every moment of it," she said. She looked him full in the face, taking in the fleshy half-moons under his eyes and the heavy lines around his mouth. It was a face she had grown to love. "But one day, Jack," she continued, "Narnia will end. My cancer will win out. This world is only a shadow of the real one. That's the whole point of *The Last Battle*, isn't it? That's why you wrote it, to convey the spiritual truth of the passing of this world into a far better one."

His eyes took on a faraway look. "Yes, Aslan's world, with brighter and more beautiful colors than we can imagine."

"What is it Jewel says in the book? 'All worlds draw to an end except Aslan's own country'? But that is the country we were really made for, Jack. What more can we ask?"

"I'll tell you what I ask," he said, kneeling beside her and wrapping his arms around her. "I ask that that bright and beautiful future country come in God's timing. But until it does, I want to make the most of every day we have together. I love you, Joy Lewis. If Narnia can't 'go on for ever and ever and ever,' I'm at least going to enjoy the days I do have." He got to his feet and tugged at her arm. "Come, let's sit in the garden. I just finished another article and can't wait to get your opinion of it."

Joy regained a significant amount of her strength, and eventually she was well enough to travel to Ireland and Greece with Jack. But the cancer returned as they knew it would, and she died on July 13, 1960. The story of their short-lived marriage and Joy's death is told in two movies by the title Shadowlands *(1984 and 1993).*

Jack turned to what he did best and wrote about his loss in A Grief Observed. *His struggle with osteoporosis continued, and he was later weakened by a heart attack. He died on November 22, 1963, just before his 65th birthday.*

C.S. Lewis's main work was as a scholar of Medieval and Renaissance literature at Cambridge, but he was better known around the world as a writer. He wrote dozens of books on a wide variety of subjects, including The Screwtape Letters, Mere Christianity, Surprised by Joy, Till We Have Faces, *and* The Problem of Pain, *but the most beloved by far are* The Chronicles of Narnia, *seven fantasy novels for children now being adapted as feature films. Many writers and other artists continue to look to his work as a model for using the God-given imagination to creatively communicate Christian truth.*

JANANI LUWUM: GOD'S HAND IS IN THIS

FEBRUARY 5, 1977. KAMPALA, UGANDA.

THE DISTANT BARKING of dogs edged into his dream and pulled him toward wakefulness. The archbishop stirred and felt for his wife beside him in the darkness. Mary was breathing softly, still asleep.

And now he thought he heard voices outside. Was it someone in the compound? In front of the house?

He sat up slowly, rubbed his eyes, and dropped his feet over the edge of the bed. The clock on the side table told him it was half-past one. He slipped on his house shoes and pushed his tired muscles off the mattress. Glancing at his wife to be sure he hadn't awakened her, he crept out of the room and past the quiet bedrooms of his children.

"Maybe it is a church emergency," he thought, moving down the dark staircase. He did not turn on the lights. He never did at night, since that would indicate he was home. These days, he needed to know who was outside before he revealed his presence.

Knocking rattled the front door, but he stopped short of opening it. Instead, he parted the curtain at a front window and peered out toward the stoop. A man stood there, his fist at the door, his profile recognizable in the hazy moonlight.

"What is Ben doing here at this time of night?" he wondered. "He must be in trouble."

"Archbishop Luwum," Ben called, knocking again. "Open the door. We have come. Open the door."

We?

He unlocked the door and cracked it open, a wedge of moonlight widening on the floor. Ben met him with frightened eyes.

"Ben, is something—?"

But three men were leaping from the shrubs, pointing black assault rifles at the archbishop. They shoved Ben through the door and he fell in the patch of pale light at Janani Luwum's feet.

"Ben!"

"I'm sorry," he moaned, licking blood from his lips. "They beat me! I'm sorry!"

And they were inside, barring the door, and waving their guns. "Archbishop Luwum?" one shouted.

The archbishop faced him, noting the military fatigues he wore. "Who are you? What have you done to my friend?"

"Where are the weapons?" was the reply. "Show us your weapons!"

Janani raised both hands. "I have no weapons. What are you talking about?"

A rifle was put to his head. He felt the cold barrel graze his cheek.

"You are lying! You are plotting to overthrow the president!"

"What?" Janani exclaimed. "President Amin knows that is not true. I'm a churchman, not a revolutionary."

"That is not what the evidence says."

Mary appeared in her nightdress, eyes wide and one hand over her mouth, with several of the children behind her. One man swiveled and pointed his rifle at her. She froze.

"Search the house!" the ranking soldier cried. They spread out across the first floor, turning over tables, dumping out drawers, ripping down curtains, emptying cabinets.

The archbishop hauled Ben from the floor and ran to his wife. They gathered the family and fled to the kitchen at the back of the house.

"What is happening, Janani?" Mary cried.

"I don't know. They keep asking about weapons!"

"I'm so sorry," Ben said again. He was shaking, and now that the lights had been thrown on, they could see his face was bruised and bloody. "They beat me, told me I had to get you to open the door. Oh! I'm so sorry!"

Somewhere upstairs, shattered glass rained down on a tile floor.

Janani shoved the children under the kitchen table. "But what do they want?"

"They said nothing else. They just——." Ben stopped short as a gunman appeared at the kitchen door.

"Where are they?" the angry soldier shouted. "We know you are involved in the plot against the president!"

Janani stepped between him and the others. "As I said, there are no weapons, and I don't know what plot you are talking about." He spoke evenly, his voice calm. "I am a minister of the gospel, not a military leader."

Then the gunman was in his face, shoving the rifle into his abdomen. "The president will be very unhappy about this," he said, low and threatening. He spun around and called to the others. "Check the storerooms outside!"

And they were gone.

Janani sank to a chair, and Mary threw her arms around him. Under the table, the children whimpered.

"This is all my fault, Archbishop!" Ben cried. He had slumped to the floor in shame.

Mary ran to him. "Ben, look what they did to you! Let me clean you up." She helped him to the table and moved to the sink to wet a towel.

Janani reached for the children, held each of them to him, and shushed them. "It's all right, now. They're gone. We're safe now."

When they were calm, he went round to each of the outside doors and windows and made sure they were locked. He had to pick his way back to the kitchen, avoiding the overturned furniture and books and papers and broken fragments of what—a lamp?— strewn through the house. Leaning against the kitchen door, he rubbed his temples in a circular motion. "It's going to take some time to clean up this mess," he groaned.

"Let me," Ben insisted, jumping up from where Mary was dabbing at his face with the cloth. "It is my fault. I will take care of it."

"It is not your fault," Mary chided. "They forced you. And I think it would be wise for you to lie down."

But he refused, and together they began to put the house in order.

Hours later, when Ben had gone home, and the babies had been put back in bed, and the older children were busy reshelving books and sorting papers, Mary pulled Janani back into the kitchen.

"What are we going to do?" she whispered hoarsely. "Idi Amin is a danger to you, to the church, to all Uganda!"

That had been growing clearer day by day. But what could be done about it? "He is an unstable man, Mary."

"That is why you cannot keep opposing him!" She closed her eyes and took a deep breath. "I know you are trying to do what is right, to respect his position while holding him accountable for his actions. But he has killed thousands of people just because they might be plotting against him! If he believes you are supporting the Acholi soldiers, he will kill you. What am I to tell your children if he succeeds?"

He sighed. "I don't think it matters who I do or don't support. Apparently everyone is an enemy."

"But you are the archbishop of Uganda, Rwanda, Burundi, and Boga-Zaire! The highest-ranking Anglican cleric!"

He shook his head. "That means nothing to him. He has been attacking all religious leaders—Anglican, Catholic, even his own Muslims."

She stroked his arm through his cotton pajamas, her voice faraway. "People keep disappearing, bodies found floating in rivers." She jerked around and met his eyes. "Why do so many think he is returning Uganda to the people? Are they blind?"

He turned away and stared thoughtfully at the far wall, where the normally tidy pantry shelves were now a disarray of hastily-retrieved tins and boxes. When he faced her again, his jaw was set. "I think I need to ask him directly what tonight was about. It is only right that I not make assumptions, but give him a chance to tell me it was a mistake."

It took him a moment to locate a particular notebook. Flipping it open, he slid out a sheet of paper. "Here is the direct phone number the president gave me the last time I asked him to demonstrate his commitment to his clergy. I will call him myself."

Mary's bloodshot eyes widened, but she said no more as he went to make the call. Banging around the kitchen, she collected a few things to start breakfast. She hadn't gotten far when he returned.

"That was quick," she said, putting down a frying pan. "What did he say?"

"Nothing! I was told he was 'unavailable.'" He crumpled the worthless paper and tossed it in the bin, then threw himself into a chair with his head in his hands. He began to run his thumbs over the tight black curls above his ears.

To Mary, it was his most common sign of distress. Wordlessly, she wrapped her arms around him, kissed his cheek, and went back to making breakfast.

Word spread quickly that President Amin suspected the bishops of revolutionary action. The Bishop of Bukedi was his second target, security officers searching his home less than twenty-four hours after they'd been at the Luwums. Janani called an immediate meeting of the House of Bishops.

They gathered at Namirembe Cathedral, near Janani's house. As he made his way up the hill, he squinted at the glare off the impressive dome atop the cathedral, brilliant under the mid-day African sun. Trees shaded part of the long stone staircase that rambled up the grass, but at the top, the building's red bricks almost visibly radiated heat. The archbishop was glad for the instant cool that enveloped him as he stepped through the front arch.

His friend, Bishop Festo Kivengere, was waiting for him and blotting his forehead. "It is a hot day, brother."

"It gets hotter every day."

Festo frowned. "So it appears." He nodded to another bishop coming in, and led his friend to a private alcove a few steps away. "I just want to urge you to be careful," he said, his voice low. "Remember my appeal to Amin a few years ago?"

How could he forget? He nodded.

"He put the men I tried to save at the firing squad anyway."

Janani sighed. "I know. It was a terrible injustice."

"And now I spoke against him on the radio the other day. Did you hear it? I reminded all my hearers that life is precious, and charged the government not to abuse the power God gave them." He swallowed. "So I'm certain we are in his sights now, if we weren't before."

He nodded again. "Yes, and especially me. He is petrified that Acholi rebels will overthrow him, and since I was born in one of their villages——." He stopped. "But while I have the opportunity, I will preach the gospel."

"That is the key. We must remind him that we are Christians, that our allegiance is not to our native tribes but to the church of Christ. We are just trying to minister to those caught in the middle of this chaos."

Janani gave him a wry smile. "But as they say, when two elephants fight, it is the grass that suffers! Let's go in and see what wisdom our brothers have to share."

They joined the others in one of the cathedral's classrooms. When all seventeen bishops had arrived, Janani opened the meeting, and very quickly, the discussion became heated. Each bishop had his own concerns and did not want to bring down any unnecessary government wrath. Things were bad enough!

Eventually, the archbishop stood again and raised a hand for silence. "My brothers, we are being threatened. It is a serious dishonor to our God and to his people, one that he does not take lightly. Nor should we. But, for now, we also have the opportunity to plead with our president. With God as our witness, we must remind President Amin of his duty to run a just and moral government."

The bishops murmured their assent.

Festo stood at his chair. "And there is more. We are prepared to condemn him, but are we prepared to forgive him? What if the president responds to our plea?"

"He is not going to ask for forgiveness!" cried one of the bishops.

"Most likely not," Festo admitted. "But we must pray that he will. And if he does—we must immediately grant it."

The room was silent.

"Bishop Kivengere speaks truth," Janani said quietly. "Are we in agreement?"

Their internal struggles showed on their faces, but each bishop found the courage to nod his agreement. Janani sat down again, and they began the difficult task of composing a letter. It was hard to decide just what to say. In the end, they decided they must be forceful but respectful.

The letter began with the long string of honorary titles the president had given himself. Then it continued:

> We, the Archbishop and the Bishops of the Province of Uganda, Rwanda, Burundi and Boga-Zaire, meeting at Namirembe on Tuesday, 8 February, 1977, ask you to listen to our most deeply felt concern for the church and the welfare of the people whom we serve under your care.
>
> We want to tell you of our shock at the recent searches of our homes, and protest this treatment. You have said on other occasions that religious leaders have a welcome role in this country. You have demonstrated this in the past, and for that we are grateful. But now you are acting against your promise. The muzzle of the gun that was pointed at the Archbishop's stomach is, by these actions, being pointed at every Christian in these territories. This is neither right nor wise.
>
> We are grateful for the opportunity to bring these grievances and concerns to you. We beg you to give them due consideration.

They took turns signing the letter, and then left the room in groups of two and three. When they were alone, Janani turned to Festo and said, "Well, my friend, we have made our stand."

The bishop clapped his fellow churchman on the back. "And now we wait for his response. Be well, brother. I will be in touch."

Janani set out across the lawn and made his way down the steps. When he reached the road, he heard a car engine start. He didn't see anyone following him, but when he turned into the long driveway leading toward his house, he heard the car again. He looked back just as a black car stepped on the gas and sped past. The driver was wearing the dark glasses of Amin's security force.

Apparently, the president was keeping a close eye on him.

Janani and Festo did not have to wait long for a response. Only a few days after the meeting of the House of Bishops, President Amin published an open letter in the state newspaper, accusing the archbishop of conspiring against him. The same day, Janani received an official summons to meet with the president at his State House in nearby Entebbe.

When Amin's escort arrived to pick up Janani, Mary insisted she go along.

"Should this be the house of a murderer?" she whispered in her husband's ear as the driver pulled the car around the circular drive and got out to open their door.

The sprawling two-story building was lined all across the front and both wings with a wide veranda supported by stately white pillars. The inside was even more luxurious. Ornate chandeliers hung from the high, decorated ceilings. Heavy draperies adorned the windows. Mahogany tables and antique chairs were stationed at intervals across floors so highly polished that Mary could see her reflection in them. She turned to make another comment to her husband, but one of the president's aides approached.

"This way," he said. They followed him to a spacious second-floor parlor where the president was waiting for them.

He was dressed in his military uniform, and the expanse of drab green emphasized his unusual height and girth. He stretched out his meaty hand with a broad smile. "Welcome, Archbishop!" he cried. "Please, come in."

Then he noticed Mary standing behind her husband. Surprise flickered in his eyes, but he took her hand like a gentleman. "What a pleasure to see you, Mrs. Luwum! Isn't Lake Victoria beautiful this time of year?"

"Yes, it is." She withdrew her hand quickly, her eyes scanning his body, alert for a change in manner that might signal trouble.

But he misinterpreted her glance. "Yes, I am a large man, and strong," he said, smiling, and curling his bicep so it bulged. He gave Janani a meaningful look. "This is how I defeat my opponents."

He laughed suddenly, a great booming noise that wasn't at all friendly and somehow made them both feel more uneasy. But the moment passed, and he led them to a bank of leather armchairs under a tall window. A low table was set with a beautiful silver coffee service, and the steam rising from the pot indicated it was fresh.

"Please, Mrs. Luwum. Enjoy some refreshment," Amin said with a polite bow. "I won't keep your husband long."

Mary hesitated to sit, but Janani nodded to her that it was a good idea. The president's aide reached to pour her a cup of coffee, and she glanced behind her chair at the window. In the garden below, a fountain spilled into a wide basin circled with flowering shrubs. But she was too nervous to enjoy the view. The aide left, and she picked up her cup, holding it in her lap as she kept a watchful eye on her husband.

Across the long room, Amin and Janani were walking slowly. As their voices rose, snatches of their conversation drifted toward the coffee table.

"Yes, I did read your letter," the president was saying. "And of course I am sorry for your discomfort."

"But why did you ransack my home? And why are your men still following me? I have done nothing to invite your suspicion."

Amin shook his head with good humor. "Now, now, Archbishop. Saying that you do not support the rebels does not make it true. They come from your hometown. How could you not support them?"

Janani spread his hands. "Because my allegiance is not to my native village. It is to Jesus Christ. I'm a minister of the gospel, not a political revolutionary."

The president halted and leaned in with an expression completely changed. It was as though he had exiled his humor to a distant land. Janani felt his hot breath on his nose. "Where are they?" the president growled. "Where are the weapons you got from the rebels?"

The archbishop refused to step backwards, though he longed to put some distance between them. Instead, he took a breath and said, "Your Excellency, I have no weapons. I do not store weapons. I do not trade in weapons. I am a minister of the gospel, and thus I keep only the Word of God and the love of Christ."

"That is a lie!" Amin shouted.

Mary banged her coffee cup on the tray and slid to the edge of her seat.

"That is a lie," Amin said again, this time low and threatening.

The two men stared at each other for a long minute, neither flinching. Then the president whispered, "I hope you are telling the truth, Archbishop. It would be wise for you to stick to religious things and leave war to the warriors."

Janani said nothing, and suddenly Amin slapped him on the back. "Come! We must have a photo taken together." He pounded on a door in the paneled wall and instantly a photographer stepped through it with his camera in hand.

Startled, Janani frowned. "A photo! Why?"

"Oh, some people think you are dead. They think I've killed you or jailed you." He shrugged his shoulders. "These vicious rumors happen all the time. Let's go out on this balcony and get a nice picture in the sun."

With a swift movement, Janani was swept outside. Just before the flash popped, he saw that the president had welcomed his smile back to its homeland, his grin all big white teeth.

And the Luwums were sent home.

Two days later, Janani received a letter with the president's signature, stating that all the religious leaders of the country were being called to a large mid-day rally in Kampala. The Anglican bishops gathered at the cathedral to pray before they left.

"What is this about?" Festo asked when they had taken their seats.

"Perhaps Amin is just gathering his enemies in one place to make it easier to kill us!" said a fellow bishop.

"Please, brothers," Janani insisted, "be calm. I was at the State House earlier this week and he let me go home. He says he just wants us to voice our concerns."

"He has murdered thousands of Ugandans in cold blood. Why would he not do the same to us?"

"I understand your concern, but to be honest, if anyone is in danger here, it is probably me. We should bring that concern before God now. And then we will go to the rally, where we will show Jesus to the president."

They prayed together for a long time, and when they were done, Festo took his friend by the shoulder. "Doesn't this strike you as a trap?" he whispered.

Janani looked away. "It does have that scent, yes. There is a good chance I will not come home from this meeting."

"Then why go, brother?"

"I wouldn't blame anyone else for refusing to go. But I feel strongly that, in my position, I must go. I represent Christ to the believers in our congregations, and if I cannot face adversity, I am not worthy to wear the collar that identifies me as his servant."

Festo sighed and nodded, and sent him to find Mary.

And she had the same question as Festo. "How can you go? He is a madman! We saw that again just two days ago." Her black eyes flashed, with fear or anger. Janani knew her well enough to conclude it was both.

"Don't do this to your family!" she demanded. "There is no shame in fleeing the country."

He took her into his arms and kissed the top of her head. "He let me go the other day, remember? Why assume he won't do it again?"

She pulled away. "I was with you. Perhaps he didn't want to have to kill both of us."

"Well, then I'll certainly be safe this time," he said, drawing her back into his embrace. "Today he'll have an entire hall full of witnesses."

She wasn't convinced. "I will be waiting here, Janani Luwum. At a moment's notice, send for help. I'll take up arms myself if I have to!"

"I will," he promised. "Pray for us."

When the bishops arrived at the conference center as ordered, they were escorted into a large hall. Immediately, they knew something was wrong. A crowd of soldiers filled the seats, and at the front of the auditorium stood a pile of weapons, presumably confiscated from the rebels. The vice president stood beside it.

The escorts turned guns on the bishops, ordered them to keep silent, and led them down front. There the vice president commanded that the prisoners be brought out. Two men that the bishops recognized as high-ranking cabinet members were paraded before the noisy crowd, while the vice president read confessions of their treasonous activities. The confessions claimed that the cabinet officials had stashed weapons for the purpose of removing President Amin from power.

Janani and Festo stared at each other.

And then one of the guards shoved the archbishop toward the vice president. "Don't say a word," the guard warned him under his breath. "You're still not allowed to speak."

Janani stood before the vice president, who held up a file of papers. "This document in my hands is a confession, signed by Anglican Archbishop Janani Luwum, stating that he participated in this conspiracy to overthrow the president," the official shouted. He turned to his prisoner. "Isn't this true, Mr. Luwum?"

Janani said nothing, the guard's rifle poking at his back. But he shook his head in disagreement.

"This man is accused of being a traitor," the vice president continued. "What should we do with a traitor?"

"Kill him!" shouted the soldiers. "Kill him!"

The vice president raised his arms in a grand gesture. "Hear, hear, let's have order! No Ugandan citizen will be executed without a fair trial. In light of the evidence presented here, the archbishop will stand trial for treason. We will leave it to the military tribunal to see justice done."

With that, he dismissed the crowd, and the bishops were rounded up into a small room to wait for instructions. They beat on the walls, demanding to be set free, and fell to praying with loud voices.

And an hour later, two officers appeared at the door. "His Excellency wants to see you, Archbishop."

Janani moved toward the door.

Festo jumped up to follow. "I'll go with you!"

The guard stopped him with a rifle. "No, the rest of you are free to go. The archbishop will go on alone."

Janani turned and regarded his fellow bishops with sad eyes. "Do not be afraid, brothers," he said. "God's hand is in this."

They marched him away, leaving the door open. The clergymen scattered. Festo headed to the Luwum house as fast as he could go.

Janani was led to a cell where several political prisoners awaited their execution. He knew he didn't have long, so he immediately turned to them and asked to pray with them.

A few minutes later, the guards returned and took him to yet another cell. But this one was different. This one held two wooden stools—and the bloodied bodies of the two cabinet members from the auditorium. He rushed to them, but it was too late. They were dead.

He turned back to the guards to protest, but a new figure stood in the door. It was President Amin, and he was smiling as though he had come to discipline a child for a naughty but amusing prank. "Archbishop Luwum, my vice president tells me you have confessed to trying to overthrow me."

Janani stared him down. "Then your vice president is a liar and should be removed from office."

Amin held up a sheet of paper. "Oh, come now! I have your confession right here."

"I have signed no confession."

"But you are about to." He smiled, pulled a pen from his shirt pocket, and held it and the paper out to his prisoner.

Janani ignored them.

Amin's smile disappeared. He nodded to a guard, who struck the archbishop in the back with the butt of his rifle, knocking him to the ground, and then began to kick him.

"Stop!" the president barked. He was all smiles again, holding out the paper, and waiting patiently while Janani clutched at his side, coughing.

"No need to play this game, Archbishop. It can all go away if you just sign this confession."

Janani looked up from the floor, and shook his head defiantly. Blood trickled down his chin. "That would be lying, and I will not lie. I am a minister of the gospel."

"This paper says you are a conspirator against the God-ordained government. That doesn't sound like the position of a holy, non-lying preacher."

The prisoner did not respond.

"Confess and you will be spared!" Amin shouted.

"I confess Christ and Christ alone," Janani said from the floor. "Do you know Christ, Your Excellency? Because he knows you."

Amin threw aside the paper and brought his boot down hard on the archbishop's neck.

Janani cried out in pain.

"I think you have forgotten your place," Amin said brightly. "Perhaps it would be polite of me to remind you that I am the president and you are my prisoner." He waited for a response.

Janani's eyes were closed, but his lips were moving.

"What did you say, Mr. Archbishop?" The president laughed and put his head closer to the prisoner's. "I have not cut out your tongue yet. You may still speak."

"Father, forgive them," Janani whispered, "for they know not what they do."

Amin's smile faded like the sun being swallowed by a dark cloud. A storm of rage burst across his face, thunder rising from his chest. With a roar, he kicked a stool across the room, where it splintered against the wall, and reached for his pistol.

On Namirembe Hill, Festo parked his car outside the archbishop's house and ran to the door. It flew open before he could knock.

"Where's Janani?" Mary said. "Why isn't he with you? Where is he?"

Festo reached for her. "He's been arrested," he said gently. "I tried to go with him, but they would not let me."

She shrugged off his hands violently and yanked her car keys from a cabinet.

"Mary," he said. "No, you can't go. Mary! They won't let you see him!"

But she was already on her way to the car. In seconds, it was flying out the gate, leaving a haze of red dust in its wake.

Festo sank down on the stoop, legs trembling. When he had recovered himself, he went inside to use the phone. But he was back on the stoop waiting when she returned an hour later, her face streaked with tears. She ran to him.

"They wouldn't let me in!" she sobbed. "Festo, they turned their guns on me and ordered me to leave!"

He took her in his arms. "Shh, Mary, it's all right. Come inside. A few people from the church are here to pray with us. We must pray! Only God knows what has happened."

All evening, church friends arrived at the door, having heard the news about the archbishop's arrest. They brought food and brewed tea and distracted the children. And many stayed all night, praying loudly in the living room.

They were still on their knees in the morning when a stricken friend rushed into the house, a newspaper clenched in his hand. Mary snatched it, and Festo jumped to read over her shoulder.

Across the top of the page, the bold headline proclaimed: "Archbishop Killed in Car Crash." Below was a blurred photo of a mangled Range Rover.

"No!" she screamed, and fell to her knees, wailing.

Festo rapidly scanned the article. It said that Janani and two cabinet members had been detained on charges of conspiracy, and that on the way to prison where they would await trial, they tried to overpower their driver. The vehicle they were riding in crashed into a car. All three passengers were killed, and the driver was wounded.

"Not true," he mumbled. "This is not true! This photo looks just like the one in another story a few weeks ago—about the 'accidental' death of another person who opposed Amin!"

But Mary wasn't listening. She was weeping on the floor, her children in her arms, the church women surrounding her.

Festo sat down beside them and waited. When Mary had run out of tears for the time being, and the other women had taken the children into the other room to rock them, he reached out and took her hand.

"I am so sorry, Mary. So sorry! Janani was the very best man, and a remarkable leader. I want you to know the last thing he said to me."

She said nothing, but turned her swollen eyes on him.

"He said, 'Do not be afraid. God's hand is in this.' God's almighty hand, Mary. We're not going to have much time to grieve together, for I fear we will all soon be separated. But whatever happens, he wanted us to remember to trust in God's almighty hand."

She nodded. And their friends all came together then, and formed a circle around her, and began to pray again.

Janani's body was sent back to his native village to be buried, according to local custom. But his coffin was sealed. Unable to dig his grave before dark, the soldiers who delivered the casket left it in the church overnight, and Janani's relatives took the opportunity to pry it open. They found his body covered with tire tracks—and riddled with bullets. Many believed Idi Amin pulled the trigger himself.

In Kampala, 45,000 people gathered for the archbishop's memorial service. But the Luwum and Kivengere families were not there. The local Christians had insisted they flee, and they had escaped over the mountains.

Idi Amin ruled with terror from 1971-1979 and was finally forced out of power and into exile in Libya. He unsuccessfully tried to regain power in 1989. Later he settled in Saudi Arabia, where he died in 2003 without serving a day in prison for his crimes.

After his escape, Bishop Festo Kivengere traveled the world, calling attention to the atrocities Amin had committed. His book I Love Idi Amin *shook up the international community. He argued that since Jesus asked the Father to forgive those who crucified him, Ugandan Christians were obligated to love Amin even though he was evil. Amin became known as "the Hitler of Africa"; Festo Kivengere became known as "the Billy Graham of Africa."*

A statue of Janani Luwum can be found with those of other twentieth-century martyrs outside Westminster Abbey in London.

⊕THER ⨁ODERN CHRISTIANS

THE CHARACTERS IN this book are not the only significant Christians of the modern era. Below is a brief look at just a few of the many others.

Samuel Ajayi Crowther (1809-1891) was abducted at age twelve and sold into the slave trade. He was rescued by the British Navy and brought to Freetown, Sierra Leone. Cared for by missionaries, he became a Christian and eventually went to school in England. He was ordained as the first African Bishop of the Anglican Church in 1864.

William Booth (1829-1912) was born in Britain and originally worked as a pawnbroker. After his conversion, he became a Methodist pastor and traveling evangelist. In 1865, he and his wife, **Catherine** (1829-1890), opened the evangelistic society and soup kitchen now known as The Salvation Army, establishing chapters in 58 countries during his lifetime.

C.H. Spurgeon (1834-1892) was a Baptist preacher in Britain who, at the age of 19, became pastor of New Park Street Chapel in London. He was known as "the prince of preachers" for his clear speaking style, and in his lifetime preached nearly 3600 sermons. He also supported the work of Hudson Taylor and George Müller, founded a pastor's college and an orphanage, and published dozens of commentaries and other books.

Amanda Berry Smith (1837-1915) was born in Maryland to a slave family. She became a single mother when her husband was killed in the American Civil War, and worked as a cook and washerwoman to support her family and buy her sisters' freedom. Later she was invited to England to speak about her faith, where she became a popular evangelist. She also founded an orphanage in Chicago.

Abraham Kuyper (1837-1920) was a Dutch theological reformer and politician. In 1862 he became a pastor, and in 1880 he founded the Free University in Amsterdam, where he taught theology. He also served as a Member of Parliament before being elected as Prime Minister of the Netherlands from 1901-1905.

Amy Carmichael (1867-1951) grew up in Ireland and became a missionary after hearing Hudson Taylor speak in 1887. She labored in India for 55 years, rescuing girls from temple prostitution and other abuse, and founding the Dohnavur Fellowship which eventually cared for 1000 children. Out of respect for her adopted country, she always wore Indian dress. A prolific writer, she published many devotional books that would inspire later Christians, including Jim Elliot.

G.K. Chesterton (1874-1936) was a British journalist whose witty books on a variety of subjects gave him a wide readership. He was known for applying Christian principles to issues of society and government in a way that turned ideas on their heads, making him one of the most-quoted Christian writers ever. Among his many famous books are *Orthodoxy* and *The Man Who Was Thursday*.

Karl Barth (1886-1968) has been called by friends and foes as the greatest theologian of the twentieth century. His 9,000-page

Church Dogmatics has something to do with it! This Swiss theologian was a professor to Dietrich Bonhoeffer and a founder of the "Confessing Church" in Germany during the time of Nazi power. His ideas continue to spur debate.

Corrie ten Boom (1892-1983) became, in 1922, the first licensed female watchmaker in the Netherlands. She and her family believed that as Christians it was their duty to hide Jews during World War II, and their home became a key stop in the Dutch Underground. In 1944, her entire family was arrested by the Nazis and her father and sister died in concentration camps. She preserved their stories in her autobiography, *The Hiding Place*.

Richard Niebuhr (1894-1962) was a leading American Protestant theologian and an ordained minister in the Evangelical Synod (later the German Reformed Church in America). He earned his Ph.D. in religion from Yale University in 1924 and taught at several schools over his lifetime. His 1951 book *Christ and Culture* remains a favorite of many Christians.

Gladys Aylward (1902-1970) was born to a poor British family and worked as a maid to pay for her passage to China. There she served the governor as a "foot inspector," enforcing new laws against the ancient practice of female foot-binding. She also managed an inn, where travelers stopped for hot meals and gospel stories. When Japan invaded in 1938, she secretly guided nearly 100 children across the mountains to safety.

Richard Wurmbrand (1909-2001) was a Romanian pastor who spent a total of fourteen years in prison, including three in solitary confinement, for his stance against Communism. In 1967, with his wife, **Sabina** (1913-2000), who was also imprisoned for serving in the underground church, he founded The Voice of the Martyrs, an organization dedicated to assisting and communicating on behalf of persecuted Christians around the world.

Francis Schaeffer (1912-1984) was an American pastor and philosopher. He is best known as the author of numerous books, especially those on "Christian apologetics," and as the founder of L'Abri, a community for Christian study in Switzerland.

Billy Graham (1918-) is an American evangelist, author, and spiritual advisor to multiple U.S. presidents. In 1950 he founded the Billy Graham Evangelistic Association, with magazine, film, radio, and college ministries. Since 1948, he has conducted more than 40 evangelistic "crusades" with mass audiences, and in his lifetime has preached to live audiences totaling more than 215 million people—more than any preacher in history.

Nate Saint (1923-1956), **Roger Youderian** (1924-1956), **Jim Elliot** (1927-1956), **Ed McCully** (1927-1956), and **Pete Fleming** (1928-1956) were American missionaries martyred by Huaorani Indians in Ecuador. Their deaths made world news and inspired many other young people to follow their call to foreign missions.

J.I.Packer (1926-) is a highly influential Evangelical theologian. He was born in England and earned his Ph.D at Oxford, where he dedicated his life to serving the church. He is known worldwide as a professor, writer, and speaker, and served as a general editor for the English Standard Version of the Bible. Today he regularly calls Anglicans to stand firm on orthodox Protestant doctrines.

Martin Luther King, Jr. (1929-1968) was a Baptist pastor and leader of the American Civil Rights Movement, and the youngest man to receive the Nobel Peace Prize. A believer in change through nonviolence, his "I have a Dream" speech delivered in Washington D.C. inspired generations around the world. He was assassinated in 1968 in Memphis, Tennessee.

Charles Colson (1931-) was known as the "hatchet man" for former American President Richard Nixon during the infamous Watergate Scandal. When he became a Christian he pled guilty to charges of obstructing justice and served time in prison. That experience opened his eyes to the perils of prison life and led him to start Prison Fellowship in 1976. He is a well-known radio host, writer, and cultural critic.

Mark A. Noll (1946-) is an American Evangelical historian whose books have broadened the world's understanding of Evangelicalism and raised the expectations and quality of Evangelical scholarship. In 2005 he was named one of the "25 most influential Evangelicals" by *Time Magazine*.

THE FUTURE LIVES

THE TWO THOUSAND-YEAR story of Christianity is an amazing one! It began in the most fragile way possible, with a newborn baby in a manger. Yet Christ and his first hand-picked disciples shook the foundations of souls and governments. That first generation of Christians had a tremendous task ahead of them, didn't they? In times of peril and times of peace, they worshiped their Savior as faithfully as they knew how. And they embraced his commission of taking his gospel to the whole world. Some like Polycarp and Cyprian faced the lions or lost their heads. Others like Athanasius and the Great Cappadocians set out to understand and defend the doctrines of *God as trinity* and a *divine-human Christ*. Still others like Jerome and Paula and Benedict of Nursia built *monastic* communities, where Christians could meditate in seclusion and offer caring services to the poor. The religion of Christ began to take on a new shape.

During the Middle Ages, Christianity had both bright and dark moments. It saw monks and mystics, popes and princes, who all struggled to live out their faith in harsh and confusing times. The church went to war, delivering death and great disappointment. But the church also developed hospitals and universities, and raised dynamic theologians like Thomas Aquinas and Bernard of Clairvaux. Brave souls like Boniface, Constantine, and Methodius were eager to take the gospel to foreign lands, or like Francis were willing to forsake everything for a pure life, or like Catherine of Sienna, John Wyclif, and John Huss stepped forward to challenge a corrupt church.

Because of them, a new generation of reformers rose up with courage and conviction. Some like Erasmus tried to work within the church to bring change, while others like Martin Luther and Menno Simons and John Calvin found room to exercise their beliefs only outside of the established church. Disagreements among them often led to tragic circumstances. But whether through peaceful means, like Katherine Parr, or by battle like Jeanne d'Albret, many devoted themselves to the cause of freedom to worship according to their consciences. Like John Bunyan, some paid the price of prison, while others like William Bradford paid the price of lost homelands, crossing the sea so they could start over in new communities.

And others followed in the footsteps of these first Protestants. John Wesley and Jonathan Edwards reminded Christians that *conversion* meant a true change in the soul, a genuine love for God. Their preaching inspired others to take Jesus to still-unreached lands. And so Liang Fa labored in China, William Carey in India, David Livingstone in Africa, and Fidelia Fiske in Iran. Their preaching also inspired people to take Jesus to the despairing places back home. So Elizabeth Fry fought for justice for prisoners, and William Wilberforce and Harriet Beecher Stowe fought for justice for slaves. Wherever they served, their tender hearts and strong hands offered God's mercy to a world torn by sin.

And those stories carried over to yet later generations, to the people we met in this book. These stories tell of the ongoing proclamation of the enduring gospel of Christ, of followers of Jesus continuing the errand to rescue and redeem their fellow human beings from spiritual and physical danger. Working together, they saw how the ancient gospel of Jesus still meets the needs of an ever-changing world.

And in this world of new challenges, we can be certain of even more opportunities to come.

You might be too young to remember this, but a world-changing event happened in the very recent past. On September 11, 2001, in the name of the Islamic religion, *terrorists* flew two commercial airliners into the Twin Towers in New York City, and one into the Pentagon in Washington D.C., and crashed another in a field near Shanksville, Pennsylvania. Instantly, the world began thinking differently about religion. And that wasn't the only attack in the name of religion. On July 7, 2005, terrorists bombed the London public transport system during rush hour. And think of what you know about the Middle East, where nearly every day a bomb goes off in the name of one religion or another. These events have made a lot of people believe that religion—any religion—leads to evil actions. As a result, *atheists* (people who do not believe God exists) have started to challenge Christianity with more boldness than ever before. Christians are now seeking the best ways to answer the claim that the world no longer needs faith.

Terrorism and atheism are not the only challenges today's church faces. We also see challenges as a result of science. Albert Einstein (1879-1955) completely changed the way we understand the physical universe in which we live—and the rest of the twentieth century has just been trying to catch up with him! Modern science has given us new life-saving medicines and sent us to the moon. Without these scientific advances, we would not have cell phones, MRI machines, or the International Space Station. But with new knowledge always comes new problems. Now Christians are debating the morality of, for example, *human cloning* and *stem cell research*. It is likely we'll be discussing these issues for many years to come.

So the world changes, but in some ways the world also remains the same. The unspeakable *genocide* in Darfur reminds us that widespread evil is not a thing of the past. For every tyrant removed from power, another rises up to take his place. Natural disasters like earthquakes and hurricanes will keep snuffing out lives. But it is wise to remember that our sad world is also fresh with new possibilities. These challenges give us new opportunities for ministry, new ways of communicating the gospel and working for justice. Just think—it is possible that you might be one of the first missionaries to the first human colony on Mars!

When we look back at previous generations of Christians, we understand how history lives. And when we look ahead to the generations of Christians yet to come, we see that the future lives, too. Many more thrilling stories of faith and compassion and obedience will be told in the coming years.

Will yours be one of them?

AUTHOR INFORMATION

Mindy and Brandon Withrow are writers and active bloggers, and Brandon teaches historical and theological studies at Winebrenner Theological Seminary. They are both graduates of the Moody Bible Institute in Chicago; Brandon is also a graduate of Trinity Evangelical Divinity School and has a PhD in Historical Theology from Westminster Theological Seminary. They currently live in Ohio, where one of their favorite activities is reading to their nieces and nephews.

WHERE WE GOT OUR INFORMATION
AND OTHER HELPFUL RESOURCES

Bergman, Susan, ed. *Martyrs*. HarperSanFrancisco, 1996.

Bethge, Eberhard. *Dietrich Bonhoeffer: A Biography*. Fortress Press, 2000.

Bowden, John, ed. *Encyclopedia of Christianity*. Oxford University Press, 2005.

Broomhall, Marshall. *The Jubilee Story of the China Inland Mission*. Morgan and Scott, 1915.

Butler, Clementina. *Pandita Ramabai Sarasvati: Pioneer in the Movement for the Education of the Child-widow of India*. Revell, 1922. *Christian History & Biography*, issue 87.

Chung, David. *Syncretism: The Religious Context of Christian Beginnings in Korea*. SUNY Press, 2001.

Encyclopedia Britannica 2008. Encyclopedia Britannica Online School Edition.

Griffis, William Elliot. *Corea: The Hermit Nation*. Charles Scribner's Sons, 1907.

Guinness, M. Geraldine. *The Story of the China Inland Mission*, Vol. 1. Morgan and Scott, 1893.

Hardy, Arthur Sherburne. *Life and Letters of Joseph Hardy Neesima*. Houghton Mifflin, 1891.

Hooper, Walter. *C.S. Lewis: A Companion and Guide*. HarperSanFrancisco, 1996.

Hooper, Walter. *The Collected Letters of C.S. Lewis*, Vol. 3. HarperSanFrancisco, 2007.

Kang, Wi Jo. *Christ and Caesar in Modern Korea: A History of Christianity and Politics*. SUNY Press, 1997.

Kuykendall, Ralph S. *The Hawaiian Kingdom*, Vol. 3., The Kalākaua Dynasty, 1874-1893. University of Hawai'i Press, 1967.

Lewis, C.S. *The Last Battle*. Collier Books, 1970.

Linnéa, Sharon. *Princess Ka'iulani: Hope of a Nation, Heart of a People*. Eerdmans, 1999.

Maxwell David, ed., with Ingrid Lawrie. *Christianity and the African Imagination*. Brill, 2002.

Moody, William R. *D.L. Moody*. Moody Press, 2007.

Paik, L. George. *The History of Protestant Missions in Korea, 1832-1910*. Yonsei University Press, 1929.

Sankey, Ira D. *My Life and the Story of the Gospel Hymns and of Sacred Songs and Solos*. The Sunday School Times Company, 1907.

Sayer, George. *Jack: A Life of C.S. Lewis*. Crossway Books, 1988.

Slocum, Marianna, with Grace Watkins. *The Good Seed*. Promise Publishing, 1988.

Sweeney, Douglas A. *The American Evangelical Story: A History of the Movement*. Baker Academic, 2005.

Taylor, Dr. Howard and Mrs. Howard Taylor. *J. Hudson Taylor: A Biography*. Moody Press, 1965.

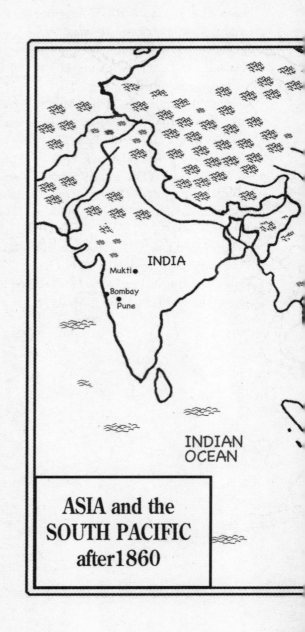

INDIA

Mukti●

Bombay
●Pune

INDIAN
OCEAN

ASIA and the SOUTH PACIFIC after 1860

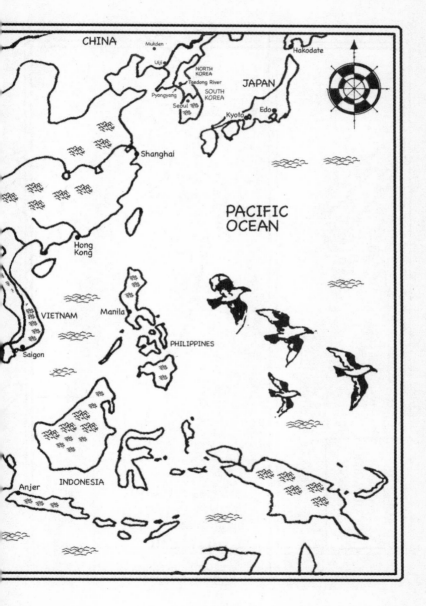

CHINA

Mukden

Uiju

NORTH
KOREA

Taedong River

Pyongyang

Seoul

SOUTH
KOREA

Hakodate

JAPAN

Kyoto

Edo

Shanghai

PACIFIC
OCEAN

Hong
Kong

VIETNAM

Manila

PHILIPPINES

Saigon

INDONESIA

Anjer

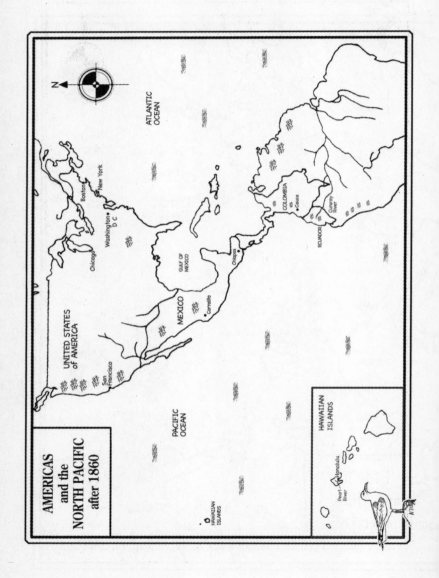

AMERICAS and the NORTH PACIFIC after 1860

ATLANTIC OCEAN

UNITED STATES of AMERICA

Boston
New York
Washington D C
Chicago
San Francisco

GULF OF MEXICO

MEXICO

Corralito
Chiapas

COLOMBIA
Cauca

ECUADOR
Curaray River

PACIFIC OCEAN

HAWAIIAN ISLANDS

HAWAIIAN ISLANDS
Pearl River
Honolulu

250

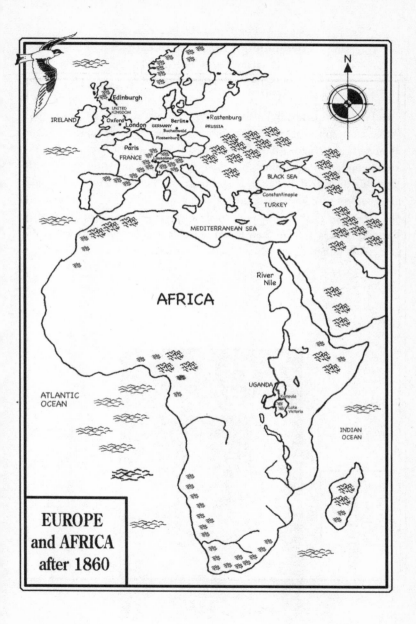

EUROPE
and AFRICA
after 1860

Peril and Peace:
Chronicles of the Ancient Church
History Lives, Volume 1
ISBN: 978-184550-082-5

Read the stories of Paul, Polycarp, Justin, Origen, Cyprian, Constantine, Athanasius, Ambrose, Augustine, John Chrysostom, Jerome, Patrick, and Benedict, and discover the roots of Christianity. In their lives you will see the young and developing church struggling and growing in a hostile and difficult world. Watch in amazement as a varied selection of people from different countries, cultures and times merge together to form the Christian church. Learn from their mistakes and errors but more importantly learn from their amazing strengths and gifts. Marvel at the incredible things accomplished by God in such a short space of time.

Monks and Mystics:
Chronicles of the Medieval Church
History Lives, Volume 2
ISBN: 978-1-84550-083-2

Read the stories of Gregory the Great, Boniface, Charlemagne, Constantine and Methodius, Vladimir, Anselm of Canterbury, Bernard of Clairvaux, Francis of Assisi, Thomas Aquinas, Catherine of Sienna, John Wyclif and John Hus. You can discover how the young Christian church moved on into another era of time to face the crusades and the spread of Islam as well as the beginnings of universities and the Reformation. Learn from their mistakes and errors but more importantly learn from their amazing strengths and gifts. Marvel at God's wonderful care of his people - the church - the Christian church.

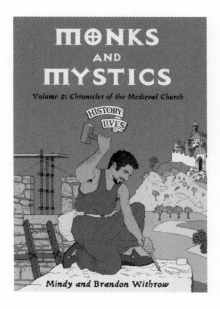

Courage and Conviction:
Chronicles of the Reformation Church
History Lives, Volume 3
ISBN: 978-1-84550-222-5

Read the stories of the reformers in the 16th and 17th centuries who changed the face of the Christian church forever. Meet the German monk, the French scholar, and the Scottish tutor who protested corruption in the church. Get to know the queens and explorers who risked everything for the freedom to worship according to their consciences. It was a time of war and upheaval, but also a time of promise and hope. From Erasmus and Luther to Katherine Parr and William Bradford, God used different personalities in different places to bring sweeping changes to church government and the way we worship. Learn from their mistakes and be encouraged by their amazing strengths and gifts.

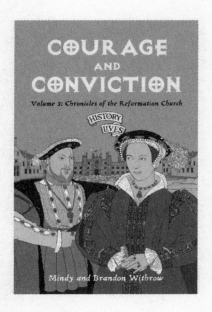

Hearts and Hands:
Chronicles of the Awakening Church
History Lives, Volume 4
ISBN: 978-1-84550-288-1

Read the stories of the gifted preachers and justice fighters who led the 1st and 2nd Great Awakenings in the 18th and 19th centuries. Meet the American preacher who started a national revival in his tiny church. Spend time with the wealthy English politician and the former American slave woman who helped abolish slavery in their countries. Get to know the missionaries who built lasting Christian communities in China, India, Africa and Iran. For the first 1700 years of the church, God's people had worked to define Christian teachings and secure their freedom to worship. Now they began to see, in a new way, how the power of the gospel should change their feelings both toward Jesus and their fellow human beings. From John Wesley and Jonathan Edwards to Elizabeth Fry and Harriet Beecher Stowe, God used the tender hearts and strong hands of his people to offer mercy to the world.

CHRISTIAN FOCUS PUBLICATIONS

Christian Focus | Christian Heritage | CF4K | Mentor

Christian Focus Publications publishes books for adults and children under its four main imprints: Christian Focus, CF4K, Mentor and Christian Heritage. Our books reflect that God's word is reliable and Jesus is the way to know him, and live for ever with him.

Our children's publication list includes a Sunday school curriculum that covers pre-school to early teens; puzzle and activity books. We also publish personal and family devotional titles, biographies and inspirational stories that children will love.

If you are looking for quality Bible teaching for children then we have an excellent range of Bible story and age specific theological books.

From pre-school to teenage fiction, we have it covered!

**Find us at our web page:
www.christianfocus.com**

CF4•K
Because you're never
too young to know Jesus